D1711742

FRANCOIS & JEAN-CLAUDE DUVALIER

FRANÇOIS & JEAN-CLAUDE DUVALIER

Erin Condit

CHELSEA HOUSE PUBLISHERS
NEW YORK
PHILADELPHIA

Chelsea House Publishers
EDITOR-IN-CHIEF: Nancy Toff
EXECUTIVE EDITOR: Remmel T. Nunn
MANAGING EDITOR: Karyn Gullen Browne
COPY CHIEF: Juliann Barbato
PICTURE EDITOR: Adrian G. Allen
ART DIRECTOR: Maria Epes
MANUFACTURING MANAGER: Gerald Levine

World Leaders—Past & Present
SENIOR EDITOR: John W. Selfridge

Staff for THE DUVALIERS
ASSOCIATE EDITOR: Jeff Klein
COPY EDITOR: Nicole Bowen
DEPUTY COPY CHIEF: Ellen Scordato
EDITORIAL ASSISTANT: Heather Lewis
PICTURE RESEARCHER: Lisa Kirchner
ASSISTANT ART DIRECTOR: Laurie Jewell
DESIGNER: David Murray
PRODUCTION COORDINATOR: Joseph Romano
COVER ILLUSTRATION: Bryn Barnard

First Printing

1   3   5   7   9   8   6   4   2

Library of Congress Cataloging-in-Publication Data

Condit, Erin.
    François & Jean-Claude Duvalier.

    (World leaders past & present)
    Bibliography: p.
    Includes index.
    Summary: Traces the lives of the man who served as president of
Haiti from 1957 to 1971 and his son who succeeded him as president
until his overthrow in 1986.
    1. Duvalier, François, 1907–1971—Juvenile literature.
2. Duvalier, Jean-Claude, 1951–   —Juvenile
literature. 3. Haiti—Politics and government—1934–1971—
Juvenile literature. 4. Haiti—Politics and government—
1971–1986—Juvenile literature. 5. Haiti—Presidents—
Biography—Juvenile literature. [1. Duvalier, François,
1907–1971. 2. Duvalier, Jean-Claude, 1951–
3. Haiti—Presidents] I. Title. II. Title: François and Jean-
Claude Duvalier. III. Series.
F1928.D86C65   1989   972.94′07′0922 [B] [920] 88-30385
ISBN 1-55546-832-2
        0-7910-0565-8 (pbk.)

Contents

JOHN ADAMS

JOHN QUINCY ADAMS

KONRAD ADENAUER

ALEXANDER THE GREAT

SALVADOR ALLENDE

MARC ANTONY

CORAZON AQUINO

YASIR ARAFAT

KING ARTHUR

HAFEZ AL-ASSAD

KEMAL ATATÜRK

ATTILA

CLEMENT ATTLEE

AUGUSTUS CAESAR

MENACHEM BEGIN

DAVID BEN-GURION

OTTO VON BISMARCK

LÉON BLUM

SIMON BOLÍVAR

CESARE BORGIA

WILLY BRANDT

LEONID BREZHNEV

JULIUS CAESAR

JOHN CALVIN

JIMMY CARTER

FIDEL CASTRO

CATHERINE THE GREAT

CHARLEMAGNE

CHIANG KAI-SHEK

WINSTON CHURCHILL

GEORGES CLEMENCEAU

CLEOPATRA

CONSTANTINE THE GREAT

HERNÁN CORTÉS

OLIVER CROMWELL

GEORGES-JACQUES
   DANTON

JEFFERSON DAVIS

MOSHE DAYAN

CHARLES DE GAULLE

EAMON DE VALERA

EUGENE DEBS

DENG XIAOPING

BENJAMIN DISRAELI

ALEXANDER DUBČEK

FRANÇOIS & JEAN-CLAUDE
   DUVALIER

DWIGHT EISENHOWER

ELEANOR OF AQUITAINE

ELIZABETH I

FAISAL

FERDINAND & ISABELLA

FRANCISCO FRANCO

BENJAMIN FRANKLIN

FREDERICK THE GREAT

INDIRA GANDHI

MOHANDAS GANDHI

GIUSEPPE GARIBALDI

AMIN & BASHIR GEMAYEL

GENGHIS KHAN

WILLIAM GLADSTONE

MIKHAIL GORBACHEV

ULYSSES S. GRANT

ERNESTO "CHE" GUEVARA

TENZIN GYATSO

ALEXANDER HAMILTON

DAG HAMMARSKJÖLD

HENRY VIII

HENRY OF NAVARRE

PAUL VON HINDENBURG

HIROHITO

ADOLF HITLER

HO CHI MINH

KING HUSSEIN

IVAN THE TERRIBLE

ANDREW JACKSON

JAMES I

WOJCIECH JARUZELSKI

THOMAS JEFFERSON

JOAN OF ARC

POPE JOHN XXIII

POPE JOHN PAUL II

LYNDON JOHNSON

BENITO JUÁREZ

JOHN KENNEDY

ROBERT KENNEDY

JOMO KENYATTA

AYATOLLAH KHOMEINI

NIKITA KHRUSHCHEV

KIM IL SUNG

MARTIN LUTHER KING, JR.

HENRY KISSINGER

KUBLAI KHAN

LAFAYETTE

ROBERT E. LEE

VLADIMIR LENIN

ABRAHAM LINCOLN

DAVID LLOYD GEORGE

LOUIS XIV

MARTIN LUTHER

JUDAS MACCABEUS

JAMES MADISON

NELSON & WINNIE
   MANDELA

MAO ZEDONG

FERDINAND MARCOS

GEORGE MARSHALL

MARY, QUEEN OF SCOTS

TOMÁŠ MASARYK

GOLDA MEIR

KLEMENS VON METTERNICH

JAMES MONROE

HOSNI MUBARAK

ROBERT MUGABE

BENITO MUSSOLINI

NAPOLÉON BONAPARTE

GAMAL ABDEL NASSER

JAWAHARLAL NEHRU

NERO

NICHOLAS II

RICHARD NIXON

KWAME NKRUMAH

DANIEL ORTEGA

MOHAMMED REZA PAHLAVI

THOMAS PAINE

CHARLES STEWART
   PARNELL

PERICLES

JUAN PERÓN

PETER THE GREAT

POL POT

MUAMMAR EL-QADDAFI

RONALD REAGAN

CARDINAL RICHELIEU

MAXIMILIEN ROBESPIERRE

ELEANOR ROOSEVELT

FRANKLIN ROOSEVELT

THEODORE ROOSEVELT

ANWAR SADAT

HAILE SELASSIE

PRINCE SIHANOUK

JAN SMUTS

JOSEPH STALIN

SUKARNO

SUN YAT-SEN

TAMERLANE

MOTHER TERESA

MARGARET THATCHER

JOSIP BROZ TITO

TOUSSAINT L'OUVERTURE

LEON TROTSKY

PIERRE TRUDEAU

HARRY TRUMAN

QUEEN VICTORIA

LECH WALESA

GEORGE WASHINGTON

CHAIM WEIZMANN

WOODROW WILSON

XERXES

EMILIANO ZAPATA

ZHOU ENLAI

CHELSEA HOUSE PUBLISHERS

ON LEADERSHIP

Arthur M. Schlesinger, jr.

LEADERSHIP, it may be said, is really what makes the world go round. Love no doubt smooths the passage; but love is a private transaction between consenting adults. Leadership is a public transaction with history. The idea of leadership affirms the capacity of individuals to move, inspire, and mobilize masses of people so that they act together in pursuit of an end. Sometimes leadership serves good purposes, sometimes bad; but whether the end is benign or evil, great leaders are those men and women who leave their personal stamp on history.

Now, the very concept of leadership implies the proposition that individuals can make a difference. This proposition has never been universally accepted. From classical times to the present day, eminent thinkers have regarded individuals as no more than the agents and pawns of larger forces, whether the gods and goddesses of the ancient world or, in the modern era, race, class, nation, the dialectic, the will of the people, the spirit of the times, history itself. Against such forces, the individual dwindles into insignificance.

So contends the thesis of historical determinism. Tolstoy's great novel *War and Peace* offers a famous statement of the case. Why, Tolstoy asked, did millions of men in the Napoleonic Wars, denying their human feelings and their common sense, move back and forth across Europe slaughtering their fellows? "The war," Tolstoy answered, "was bound to happen simply because it was bound to happen." All prior history predetermined it. As for leaders, they, Tolstoy said, "are but the labels that serve to give a name to an end and, like labels, they have the least possible connection with the event." The greater the leader, "the more conspicuous the inevitability and the predestination of every act he commits." The leader, said Tolstoy, is "the slave of history."

Determinism takes many forms. Marxism is the determinism of class. Nazism the determinism of race. But the idea of men and women as the slaves of history runs athwart the deepest human instincts. Rigid determinism abolishes the idea of human freedom—

the assumption of free choice that underlies every move we make, every word we speak, every thought we think. It abolishes the idea of human responsibility, since it is manifestly unfair to reward or punish people for actions that are by definition beyond their control. No one can live consistently by any deterministic creed. The Marxist states prove this themselves by their extreme susceptibility to the cult of leadership.

More than that, history refutes the idea that individuals make no difference. In December 1931 a British politician crossing Park Avenue in New York City between 76th and 77th Streets around 10:30 P.M. looked in the wrong direction and was knocked down by an automobile—a moment, he later recalled, of a man aghast, a world aglare: "I do not understand why I was not broken like an eggshell or squashed like a gooseberry." Fourteen months later an American politician, sitting in an open car in Miami, Florida, was fired on by an assassin; the man beside him was hit. Those who believe that individuals make no difference to history might well ponder whether the next two decades would have been the same had Mario Constasino's car killed Winston Churchill in 1931 and Giuseppe Zangara's bullet killed Franklin Roosevelt in 1933. Suppose, in addition, that Adolf Hitler had been killed in the street fighting during the Munich *Putsch* of 1923 and that Lenin had died of typhus during World War I. What would the 20th century be like now?

For better or for worse, individuals do make a difference. "The notion that a people can run itself and its affairs anonymously," wrote the philosopher William James, "is now well known to be the silliest of absurdities. Mankind does nothing save through initiatives on the part of inventors, great or small, and imitation by the rest of us—these are the sole factors in human progress. Individuals of genius show the way, and set the patterns, which common people then adopt and follow."

Leadership, James suggests, means leadership in thought as well as in action. In the long run, leaders in thought may well make the greater difference to the world. But, as Woodrow Wilson once said, "Those only are leaders of men, in the general eye, who lead in action. . . . It is at their hands that new thought gets its translation into the crude language of deeds." Leaders in thought often invent in solitude and obscurity, leaving to later generations the tasks of imitation. Leaders in action—the leaders portrayed in this series—have to be effective in their own time.

And they cannot be effective by themselves. They must act in response to the rhythms of their age. Their genius must be adapted, in a phrase of William James's, "to the receptivities of the moment." Leaders are useless without followers. "There goes the mob," said the French politician hearing a clamor in the streets. "I am their leader. I must follow them." Great leaders turn the inchoate emotions of the mob to purposes of their own. They seize on the opportunities of their time, the hopes, fears, frustrations, crises, potentialities. They succeed when events have prepared the way for them, when the community is awaiting to be aroused, when they can provide the clarifying and organizing ideas. Leadership ignites the circuit between the individual and the mass and thereby alters history.

It may alter history for better or for worse. Leaders have been responsible for the most extravagant follies and most monstrous crimes that have beset suffering humanity. They have also been vital in such gains as humanity has made in individual freedom, religious and racial tolerance, social justice, and respect for human rights.

There is no sure way to tell in advance who is going to lead for good and who for evil. But a glance at the gallery of men and women in *World Leaders—Past and Present* suggests some useful tests.

One test is this: Do leaders lead by force or by persuasion? By command or by consent? Through most of history leadership was exercised by the divine right of authority. The duty of followers was to defer and to obey. "Theirs not to reason why / Theirs but to do and die." On occasion, as with the so-called enlightened despots of the 18th century in Europe, absolutist leadership was animated by humane purposes. More often, absolutism nourished the passion for domination, land, gold, and conquest and resulted in tyranny.

The great revolution of modern times has been the revolution of equality. The idea that all people should be equal in their legal condition has undermined the old structure of authority, hierarchy, and deference. The revolution of equality has had two contrary effects on the nature of leadership. For equality, as Alexis de Tocqueville pointed out in his great study *Democracy in America,* might mean equality in servitude as well as equality in freedom.

"I know of only two methods of establishing equality in the political world," Tocqueville wrote. "Rights must be given to every citizen, or none at all to anyone . . . save one, who is the master of all." There was no middle ground "between the sovereignty of all and the absolute power of one man." In his astonishing prediction of 20th-century totalitarian dictatorship, Tocqueville explained how the revolution of equality could lead to the *"Führerprinzip"* and more terrible absolutism than the world had ever known.

But when rights are given to every citizen and the sovereignty of all is established, the problem of leadership takes a new form, becomes more exacting than ever before. It is easy to issue commands and enforce them by the rope and the stake, the concentration camp and the *gulag.* It is much harder to use argument and achievement to overcome opposition and win consent. The Founding Fathers of the United States understood the difficulty. They believed that history had given them the opportunity to decide, as Alexander Hamilton wrote in the first Federalist Paper, whether men are indeed capable of basing government on "reflection and choice, or whether they are forever destined to depend . . . on accident and force."

Government by reflection and choice called for a new style of leadership and a new quality of followership. It required leaders to be responsive to popular concerns, and it required followers to be active and informed participants in the process. Democracy does not eliminate emotion from politics; sometimes it fosters demagoguery; but it is confident that, as the greatest of democratic leaders put it, you cannot fool all of the people all of the time. It measures leadership by results and retires those who overreach or falter or fail.

It is true that in the long run despots are measured by results too. But they can postpone the day of judgment, sometimes indefinitely, and in the meantime they can do infinite harm. It is also true that democracy is no guarantee of virtue and intelligence in government, for the voice of the people is not necessarily the voice of God. But democracy, by assuring the right of opposition, offers built-in resistance to the evils inherent in absolutism. As the theologian Reinhold Niebuhr summed it up, "Man's capacity for justice makes democracy possible, but man's inclination to injustice makes democracy necessary."

A second test for leadership is the end for which power is sought. When leaders have as their goal the supremacy of a master race or the promotion of totalitarian revolution or the acquisition and exploitation of colonies or the protection of greed and privilege or the preservation of personal power, it is likely that their leadership will do little to advance the cause of humanity. When their goal is the abolition of slavery, the liberation of women, the enlargement of opportunity for the poor and powerless, the extension of equal rights to racial minorities, the defense of the freedoms of expression and opposition, it is likely that their leadership will increase the sum of human liberty and welfare.

Leaders have done great harm to the world. They have also conferred great benefits. You will find both sorts in this series. Even "good" leaders must be regarded with a certain wariness. Leaders are not demigods; they put on their trousers one leg after another just like ordinary mortals. No leader is infallible, and every leader needs to be reminded of this at regular intervals. Irreverence irritates leaders but is their salvation. Unquestioning submission corrupts leaders and demeans followers. Making a cult of a leader is always a mistake. Fortunately hero worship generates its own antidote. "Every hero," said Emerson, "becomes a bore at last."

The signal benefit the great leaders confer is to embolden the rest of us to live according to our own best selves, to be active, insistent, and resolute in affirming our own sense of things. For great leaders attest to the reality of human freedom against the supposed inevitabilities of history. And they attest to the wisdom and power that may lie within the most unlikely of us, which is why Abraham Lincoln remains the supreme example of great leadership. A great leader, said Emerson, exhibits new possibilities to all humanity. "We feed on genius. . . . Great men exist that there may be greater men."

Great leaders, in short, justify themselves by emancipating and empowering their followers. So humanity struggles to master its destiny, remembering with Alexis de Tocqueville: "It is true that around every man a fatal circle is traced beyond which he cannot pass; but within the wide verge of that circle he is powerful and free; as it is with man, so with communities."

1

The Flight

The American diplomats waiting on the darkened runway of Haiti's François Duvalier International Airport glanced at their watches, becoming increasingly tense with each passing minute. It was 2:00 A.M. on February 7, 1986. Moments earlier a huge U.S. Air Force C-141 Starlifter had touched down and roared to a stop. Now it stood on the tarmac, its engines whining in preparation for a quick take-off. But the ruler it had come to rescue was two hours late.

A day earlier Jean-Claude Duvalier, Haiti's president-for-life, had sent an urgent message to the United States embassy asking the Americans to help him and his family flee the country. Now, after weeks of bloody antigovernment riots, Duvalier's absence was cause for concern. Had the escape plan been foiled by the angry opposition to the Duvalier family's 29-year-old regime? Had the mobs calling for Duvalier's head gotten to him before he could get to the airport? The Americans standing on the runway feared the worst.

My Country is not a garbage can.
—OMAR BONGO
president of Gabon on why he refused to grant Jean-Claude Duvalier asylum.

Haitian dictator François Duvalier in May 1963. Papa Doc, as he was known, was elected president in 1957 and soon established a brutal dictatorial rule that lasted until his death in 1971. His son, Jean-Claude "Baby Doc" Duvalier, succeeded him as Haiti's president-for-life.

Jean-Claude Duvalier (at the wheel) and his wife, Michèle, arrive at the Port-au-Prince airport at 3:30 A.M. on February 7, 1986, to flee Haiti in the face of antigovernment rioting and protests. A last-minute going-away party made them three hours late for their flight to exile aboard a U.S. air force plane.

Finally, at 3:30 A.M., the headlights of a silver BMW sliced through the darkness. As the car drew close, reporters and photographers surrounded it; the glare of television lights and popping flashbulbs illuminated the interior. Sitting in the driver's seat, hunched over and gripping the wheel, was a determined 34-year-old man dressed in a dark business suit, white shirt, and tie. It was Jean-Claude Duvalier. Michèle Bennett, his stunning wife, was sitting beside him, wearing an elegant white turban. She puffed nervously on the cigarette she held between the fingers of her left hand.

The car rolled to a halt. Duvalier and his wife stepped out, bade farewell, and hurriedly boarded the cargo plane. At 3:46 A.M. the C-141 roared down the runway and climbed into the night carrying the Duvaliers and 17 close associates to a pampered exile in France.

14

Five hours after the Duvaliers fled Haiti, a six-man ruling council appointed by Jean-Claude and headed by Lt. Col. Henri Namphy, the commander of the armed forces, took over the predominantly black republic to head off what Namphy called "the frightful specter of civil war." The military had last seized power in 1957 to oversee the election of Jean-Claude's father, François "Papa Doc" Duvalier, a man who became the most powerful dictator in Haitian history and who, shortly before his death in 1971, bequeathed the title of president-for-life to his teenage son. Now, with Jean-Claude gone, Namphy assured the press that the military did not "entertain any political ambition" and "would hold elections as soon as possible," but many Haitians remained unconvinced. Several members of Namphy's new provisional government had been loyal to the Duvaliers.

The military attempted to control civil unrest in the weeks that followed Jean-Claude's ouster, but celebrating Haitians quickly turned into uncontrollable lynch mobs and looters. Rioters tore apart Papa Doc's marble-and-granite mausoleum in search of the late dictator's body. Finding that it had been removed, they closed in on the grave of one of Duvalier's associates, pulled out the corpse,

A slum in Port-au-Prince, Haiti's capital. Haiti, already the Western Hemisphere's poorest nation, became even poorer under the Duvaliers. By 1986, 90 percent of the population lived in poverty, in part because the Duvaliers had embezzled hundreds of millions of dollars in public funds.

Gaining revenge for nearly 30 years of Duvalier tyranny was the first thought of many Haitians when they learned that Baby Doc had departed. Here Haitian police try to disperse a mob attacking the home of a leader of the Tontons Macoutes, the Duvaliers' personal militia.

and ripped off its head and limbs. Angry mobs sought out and burned or hacked to death members of the Duvaliers' brutal personal militia — the infamous *Tontons Macoutes* — and killed as many as 100 Voodoo priests believed to have supported the old regime.

The ferocity of these attacks surprised few. Both Papa Doc and Jean-Claude, "Baby Doc," had stayed in power by killing their opponents — and quite often uninvolved civilians — thereby creating an atmosphere of terror that ensured absolute obedience to their rule. They used Voodoo, Haiti's widely practiced folk religion, to control believers. They further held a tight grip on the nation by maintaining the appalling poverty and ignorance of the people, all the while enriching themselves through the diversion of public money (much of it foreign aid) and the extraction of bribes and kickbacks. In the end, it was estimated that the Duvalier family had salted away as much as $900 million in foreign bank accounts while the vast majority of Haitians lived in abject poverty.

Under Duvalier rule the Western Hemisphere's poorest country became even poorer. In 1986, Haiti, which shares the island of Hispaniola with the Dominican Republic, supported its 6.2 million people on a piece of land the size of the state of Maryland. Yet much of the Caribbean nation's 10,714-square-mile territory, two-thirds of which is mountainous, could no longer produce crops or other agricultural products. As a result, farmers abandoned their useless, eroding lands and moved into cities. There the average Haitian, who in 9 out of 10 cases could not read or write, earned $350 a year — twice as much as the rural farmer, but still far below the poverty line. The capital city of Port-au-Prince had almost no drinkable water and no sewage system; yet its disease-ridden slums were home to more than half a million people. Average life expectancy was less than 45 years, 10 percent of all infants were stillborn, and at least one-third of the children under 5 years of age were dying slowly of malnutrition and associated diseases. Haiti had no mineral exports and very little fuel except for wood from the nation's few remaining stands of trees. The once-flourishing tourist industry was moribund; thousands of North Americans and Europeans who had once flocked to the island were gone, scared away by the alarming spread of AIDS among the Haitian population. This was the nation Jean-Claude Duvalier left behind.

As the blinking red lights of the C-141 carrying Duvalier receded into the dark sky, the American officials who had arranged his departure stood dumbfounded on the runway. They asked him as he had boarded the plane why he was so late in getting to the airport. Without the faintest trace of apology, Duvalier answered that he and Michèle had thrown themselves a last-minute going-away party — a lavish *coup de champagne* for friends and allies at the presidential palace. With that he dashed up the stairs, entered the plane, and flew away.

2

Legacy of Blood

Jean-Claude Duvalier had stayed in power for a decade and a half in part because of the Voodoo belief that the spirit of his dead father, the murderous and manipulative François Duvalier, was ruling the country through his son.

A truly remarkable politician, François Duvalier was the first Haitian president to harness the support of the poor black masses of the countryside, where the vast majority of the population lived and worked according to the ancient unwritten laws of the Voodoo religion. He quietly and cunningly manipulated people and events to win the presidency, immediately crushed all opposition, and embarked on a 13-year reign in which he terrorized the entire nation into absolute obedience — and even worship. Duvalier's behavior throughout was erratic and unpredictable to the point of being bizarre, yet it always produced the effect of awing the population. When, during a speech in 1963, Duvalier said, "I am already an immaterial being" and claimed that bullets could not harm him, the rapt crowd of thousands believed him.

So lovable, so tractable, so peaceful . . .
—CHRISTOPHER COLUMBUS
describing the island
of Hispaniola

A street scene in Port-au-Prince. Throughout Haiti's history the mulatto elite and the black urban poor lived in the capital while the majority of the black population lived in the countryside. François Duvalier rose to power by tapping the support of rural blacks.

Early in his career, it seemed that Duvalier was concerned with the plight of the impoverished masses and that he would try to change the course of Haitian events. But instead, he and his regime succumbed to the unending cycle of poverty and repression that has preyed upon the nation for five centuries, adding a new chapter of violence and death to Haiti's blood-soaked history.

Although Haiti was the world's first black republic and, after the United States, only the second colony in the Western Hemisphere to achieve independence, the nation never modernized. While other countries grew and progressed, Haiti remained much the same as it had been in 1791, when it first rebelled against France. In many ways the Haitian peasants of the 1980s resembled their ancestors; throughout the nation's history, the peasants have known subservience to absolute masters, whether it was the slave traders and plantation owners of the 17th and 18th centuries or the Duvaliers and other dictators of the 19th and 20th centuries.

In the 1980s, as always, the wealthy ruling class remained the five percent of the population that was predominantly white or mulatto — the term used in Haiti to denote people of mixed French and Negro blood. This elite, commonly educated in France, spoke French, followed French cultural traditions, and professed faith in the Roman Catholic church. Most of them felt far superior to the other 95 percent of the population, the black masses who, after almost 200 years of independence, remained poor, uneducated, and ignorant of the world beyond their immediate horizon.

The black majority, descendants of colonial slaves, could not speak French, even though it was Haiti's official language. They conversed only in Creole, a largely unwritten language that is a rich mixture of French, English, Dutch, Spanish, German, and West African tongues. Their religious, cultural, and societal base was rooted in the practice of Voodoo, a fascinating combination of Roman Catholicism and West African religions. This often misunderstood folk religion continues to be the un-

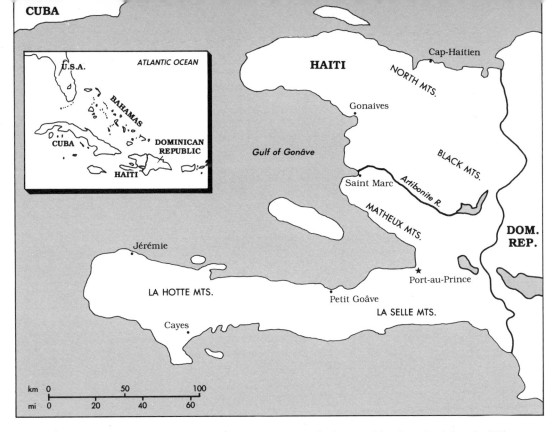

official, yet powerful, governing authority of the black majority and the creative force behind Haiti's distinctive music, dance, and art.

Because of their obvious differences in language, culture, and heritage, the two groups have led separate, socially distinct existences for almost 200 years. The peasants distrust the elite, and the elite look down upon and ignore the peasants — a situation similar to the master-slave relationship of the colonial past. To understand why this society has prevailed and how François Duvalier was able to seize and maintain power, it is necessary to examine Haiti's violent history.

One year after Christopher Columbus discovered Hispaniola in 1492 he established the first permanent colony in the New World, which led to warfare with the island's native Arawak Indians. Soon the Spanish succeeded in enslaving the Arawaks, but within a few years the Indians died out, the victims of brutality and disease. The Spaniards needed slave labor to operate the plantations they were establishing on the island, so they began to import black

Sharing the island of Hispaniola with the Spanish-speaking Dominican Republic, Haiti is a mountainous nation of 6 million people, 95 percent of whom are black and the remainder of mixed black and white, or mulatto, ancestry. It is located about 60 miles east of Cuba and 580 miles southeast of Florida.

In the 17th and 18th centuries, slave labor made Haiti, then known as Saint Domingue, the French empire's richest colony. Black slaves, brought from Africa, outnumbered white landowners by 500,000 to 70,000. During some years one-third of the black population died as a result of the slaveowners' brutality.

Africans; thus Hispaniola became the catalyst for the establishment of the slave trade between Africa and the Western Hemisphere.

During the 17th century, England, France, and Holland, refusing to accept Spain's claim to the Caribbean, sailed into the area and colonized many of the islands for their own economic gain. By 1700 France established a colony, known as Saint Domingue, in the western third of Hispaniola, which had been uninhabited since the extinction of the Arawaks. Spain's colony on the eastern portion of the island was called Santo Domingo. The two colonies would eventually become the culturally distinct, often warring nations of Haiti and the Dominican Republic.

Saint Domingue soon became the jewel of the French colonial empire and the most coveted possession of the age. The colony, with more than 500,000 African slaves, generated two-thirds of France's overseas trade, a level of productivity that surpassed the North American colonies and outranked the total annual output of all the Spanish West Indies combined. In 1789 alone, exports of Haitian sugar, cotton, indigo, coffee, cacao, and tobacco filled the holds of more than 4,000 ships.

But the fortunes made by the colony's landowners were built on the backs of hundreds of thousands of black slaves. Saint Domingue epitomized the decadent plantation societies found throughout the Caribbean, where outnumbered planters lived in constant fear of slave revolt. The slaves, confronted with endless intimidation and torture, had few options. Some escaped, some committed suicide, others endured under inhuman conditions. Field hands caught eating sugarcane were forced to wear tin muzzles while they worked. Runaways had their hamstrings cut. Workers had nails driven through their ears for the slightest infractions. Indiscriminate floggings and killings were commonplace; tens of thousands of slaves were killed or worked to death every year. The legacy of repression and brutality that began with the overseer's whip would continue in the 20th-century tactics of the Duvaliers' Tontons Macoutes.

By the late 1700s the population had become rigidly stratified according to skin color — the lighter the skin, the richer and more powerful the person. As in the rest of the Caribbean, the white planters forced slave women into their beds; the mulatto children that resulted, although born into slavery, were often freed and occasionally inherited property. Many became wealthy estate owners and slaveholders themselves. Yet, because of the shade of their skin, they were denied social and political equality by the white ruling class.

What began as a push for mulatto equality ended in the first successful slave revolt in history. Inspired by the French Revolution of 1789, with its promise of freedom and equality for all men, the slave population overran the white French colonials, whom they outnumbered seven to one. The slave uprising — prepared in secrecy by Voodoo leaders, who used drum beats to instruct their followers — began in August 1791 and soon escalated into full-scale warfare during which other colonial powers tried to conquer the rich colony for themselves. The wars would rage on for 12 savage years, and at one point 7 warring parties were fighting simultaneously: slaves, mulattoes, rich white landowners,

> *To write this Act of independence we must have a white man's skin for parchment, his skull for an inkwell, his blood for ink, and a bayonet as pen.*
> —LT. BOISROND TONNÈRE
> on the day of Haitian
> independence from France

François-Dominique Toussaint L'Ouverture, himself a slave, led Saint Domingue's slaves in an uprising that began in 1791 and ended in 1804 with the founding of the world's first black republic. In between, Toussaint's forces defeated the colony's whites and the national armies of France, Britain, and Spain.

poor whites, invading Spanish and English forces, and the French military. Alliances were numerous but fleeting, a state of affairs that would come to mark Haitian politics — particularly during the Duvalier era.

By 1794 the scales of power began to tip in favor of the slaves under the leadership of three black men of military genius: the former slaves François-Dominique Toussaint L'Ouverture, Henri Christophe, and Jean-Jacques Dessalines. Within four years the rebels would successively defeat the French, expel the British invaders, subdue the southern mulatto opposition, defeat the Spanish, and conquer Santo Domingo.

Meanwhile, the French Revolution had fallen into the hands of Napoleon Bonaparte, who tried to restore colonialism and slavery to Saint Domingue and reestablish France's empire in the Americas. In December 1801, Napoleon dispatched what was then the largest French overseas military expedition in history; the forces were led by his brother-in-law, General Charles-Victor-Emmanuel Leclerc, who had orders to stamp out the slave revolt in Saint Domingue.

The expedition succeeded in conquering the Spanish portion of the island. But except for the capture of Toussaint L'Ouverture, the blacks' brilliant general, the French campaign in Saint Domingue was a complete failure. By 1803, France had lost more than 60,000 soldiers to war and yellow fever, among them Leclerc. Because of the huge military and financial loss at Saint Domingue, Napoleon decided to sell all 800,000 square miles of the Louisiana Territory (the vaguely defined area between the Mississippi River and the Rocky Mountains) to the United States for 60 million francs — roughly 4 cents an acre.

The victorious former slaves of Saint Domingue officially proclaimed independence on New Year's Day, 1804, and renamed the country Haiti, an old Arawak word meaning "land of mountains." The impact on the world outside the new republic was monumental. It was the first time in history that slaves had successfully risen to create a new nation, and it signaled the beginning of the end of the African slave trade.

But Haiti itself remained troubled. After years of civil war in which the country's plantations and towns were repeatedly sacked and burned, the economy was in ruins, and the country's finances were drained further by the enormous expense of its conquest and control of the Spanish portion of the island from 1823 to 1844. A largely racist world wanted nothing to do with the black republic — thus lessening the nation's chances for economic recovery — and Haitians, bitter memories of colonial rule still fresh in their minds, wanted nothing to do with the world.

Although the century-long isolation that followed independence allowed Haiti to develop its Creole language and unique culture, the lack of education and of interaction with other countries spawned the miserable poverty and the bizarre political legacy that François Duvalier would one day inherit. The masses turned to subsistence farming and looked to their *houngans* (Voodoo priests) for protection and leadership, while a succession of "monarchs," "kings," and "presidents" — all dictators — took over Port-au-Prince and plundered Haiti's small public wealth. Most of these rulers were illiterate black military officers placed in power by the mulatto elite, who manipulated irregular elections for their own economic gain.

The Citadel, Henri Christophe's fortress in northern Haiti. Christophe aided Toussaint and Jean-Jacques Dessalines in the Haitian revolution; after the French captured Toussaint, Christophe had Dessalines killed and crowned himself King Henri I. He ruled for 14 years before committing suicide in 1820.

Each July, Voodoo worshipers gather at the waterfall of Ville Bonheur, which they believe harbors the spirits of both the Virgin Mary and the Voodoo snake god Damballah Ouedo. Voodoo, Haiti's most widely practiced religion, blends elements of West African animism, Roman Catholicism, and West Indian folk beliefs.

The despots who preceded Duvalier adopted the use of force and the psychology of terror from Saint Domingue's slave society as a means of controlling the people. In the 103 years between independence and the birth of François Duvalier on April 14, 1907, Haiti endured dictatorship under anywhere from 70 to 129 rulers; coups and revolts were so frequent that the exact number of rulers remains unknown.

François Duvalier's early childhood years were difficult. His father, Duval Duvalier, was a frequently unemployed black schoolteacher, born and educated on the French Caribbean island of Martinique; his Haitian mother, Uritia Abraham, worked in a bakery. The family lived in a slum only a few blocks away from the National Palace in Port-au-Prince; their small home was located on an unpaved street with open drainage ditches that doubled as sewers. Nearby merchants ran stores fronted with iron doors to withstand the destruction of Haiti's frequent revolutions, coups, and power struggles. In this environment, Duvalier learned the primitive rules that would allow him to gain and retain absolute power, the only kind that seemed to last in Haiti.

During the first eight years of Duvalier's life the presidency changed hands seven times. Every time a new president rose to power another faction would borrow money from abroad to buy the arms and munitions necessary to overthrow the government.

Not surprisingly, successive Haitian governments faced such overwhelming foreign debts that by July 1915, German, French, and American gunboats paraded in the harbor at Port-au-Prince ready to reclaim their investments.

Bankrupt, Haiti was on the verge of yet another coup. President Vilbrun Guillaume Sam, who had held office a scant 7 months, jailed 167 of his political enemies at the outset of the fighting and ordered the prison commander to kill them if the revolt succeeded. Duvalier, a quiet boy who did not play games and liked to be alone, witnessed what happened next from a window at the Lycée National, a primary and secondary school that had a clear view of the harbor and downtown Port-au-Prince.

As the revolt gathered momentum, Sam sought asylum at the French embassy. In obedience to his orders, all but five of the political prisoners were slaughtered and their remains displayed around Port-au-Prince. As families searched the capital city for the bodies of slain relatives, a rumor spread that the U.S. Marines had arrived to protect Sam. An anti-Sam mob stormed the gates of the French embassy, found Sam, impaled his body on the spiked iron fence that surrounded the compound, and tore him to pieces. Duvalier, a boy of eight, saw it all.

Sam would have been a brief footnote in Haitian history had the U.S. government not used the political unrest that followed his death as an excuse

The National Palace in Port-au-Prince. For 150 years Haitian politics reflected the nation's economic and racial divisions. The Roman Catholic, French-speaking mulatto elite controlled political power and the nation's wealth whereas the Creole-speaking, predominantly Voodoo black majority remained poor.

U.S. Marines on patrol in Haiti in 1919. In 1915 the United States invaded and occupied Haiti because it could not pay its debts to the U.S. government. One year later U.S. forces took Haiti's neighbor, the Dominican Republic, as well. The U.S. occupation of both nations lasted until 1934.

to invade Haiti. Mindful of Haiti's strategic location near the recently constructed Panama Canal, the United States landed a force of 2,000 white marines (blacks were not allowed to enlist in the Marine Corps until World War II) and occupied the country until 1934. In 1916 the marines also invaded the Dominican Republic, thus giving the United States control of the entire island. The occupations followed previous U.S. interventions in Panama, Nicaragua, and Cuba.

The marines brought progress. They built roads, sewage systems, telephone lines, telegraph systems, irrigation canals, wharves, schools, prisons, and hospitals in an attempt to bring the benefits of American development to Haiti. But to accomplish these ends they used a system of forced labor, or *corvée*, that amounted to little more than another form of slavery. The result was the same as it had been under every previous regime: new masters ruling and the masses, in effect, still slaves.

The U.S. occupation forces manipulated Haitian elections, dissolved the legislature, and trained the local police to keep dissent to a minimum. They forced the passage of a constitution — written not by Haitians but by Assistant Secretary of the U.S. Navy Franklin D. Roosevelt — and the acceptance of a treaty dissolving Haitian sovereignty. Haitians, who had resisted foreign domination since the days of colonialism, protested loudly and violently.

In 1919, while Duvalier was still attending the Lycée, he and his fellow students witnessed numerous bloody attacks on the marines by the *cacos*, peasant guerrillas who fought the U.S. occupation. Their leader was Charlemagne Péralte, a former commander of the Haitian armed forces who refused to relinquish his office, arms, and flag when U.S. troops took over. The marines offered a $2,000 reward for Péralte's life; his killer received not only the money but also the Congressional Medal of Honor. To show the peasants that their leader was dead and that resistance was useless, the marines tied Péralte's body to the door of police headquarters. The peasants thought Péralte looked like the crucified Jesus Christ.

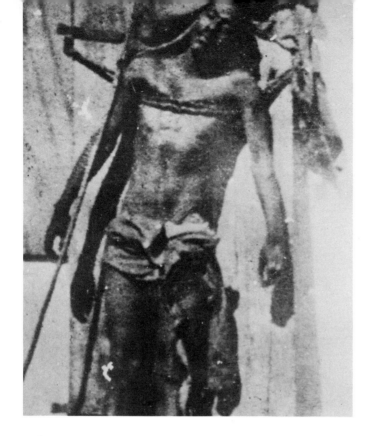

The body of Haitian guerrilla leader Charlemagne Péralte was lashed to the door of a police station by U.S. Marines in 1919. The Americans killed hundreds of Haitians, but the resistance movement united all elements of Haitian society and stimulated a new awareness of their black African roots in young intellectuals such as François Duvalier.

Soon the mulatto elite and a very small but growing group of black Haitian scholars joined the peasants in calling for an end to the U.S. occupation, particularly after the marines killed more than 3,000 Haitians during a rural insurrection in 1921–22. For the first time since independence the entire population had a common enemy. Among those urging an immediate withdrawal of U.S. troops were Duvalier's teachers at the Lycée, including Dr. Jean Price Mars, a leading Haitian ethnologist, and Dumarsais Estimé, who was destined to become one of Haiti's postoccupation presidents.

The U.S. occupation, during which the white marines treated blacks and mulattoes with unbridled racism, did little to change Haitians or Haitian life in any lasting way. But it did have one unforeseen side effect: It helped young intellectuals like Duvalier to renounce colonial French traditions and to embrace the black African cultural heritage of the masses. This new black ethnic awareness gave birth to the *Négritude* movement that would eventually propel François Duvalier to power.

3

The Rise of Papa Doc

François Duvalier's ascent to power began harmlessly and ended murderously. An extremely shy person, young Duvalier rarely spoke unless spoken to and appeared to be emotionally insecure. His early writings suggested a wish to be like Haiti's revolutionary heroes — smarter, stronger, and more powerful than everyone else. Yet physically the 19-year-old Duvalier was a short, slight, nearsighted young man, hardly the figure of power and strength that preoccupied him. He would eventually find his personal strength, acceptance, notoriety, and power in Haiti's traditional religion, Voodoo.

Voodoo formed the heart of the Haitian Négritude movement, which promoted a new nationalism that openly acknowledged the African roots of the people. At a time when the Haitian government was suppressing Voodoo and ordering peasants to swear allegiance to the Roman Catholic church, Duvalier declared Voodoo the legitimate religion of the people. It was a courageous stand and one that earned him the support of the poor black masses, whose practice of Voodooism was not only a religion but also a form of social structure and even a means of survival.

> *The peasants love their Doc.*
> —FRANÇOIS DUVALIER

François Duvalier upon becoming president in 1957. Elected as the champion of Haiti's long-oppressed black majority, Duvalier quickly created a climate of terror in which his leadership went unquestioned. He thus became the latest in a long succession of dictators to rule the Caribbean nation.

Protesters at Pont-Beudet in March 1930 demand the restoration of Haiti's legislature, the payment of reparations by the United States, and the withdrawal of U.S. forces. At the time Duvalier was a 23-year-old medical student just beginning to develop an interest in politics.

Duvalier would intelligently exploit his knowledge of Voodoo to maintain his presidency. He found that he could control his uneducated and superstitious compatriots by spreading rumors about his great powers, his secret Voodoo ceremonies, and his sacrifices to the spirits. With the support of the masses, Duvalier would counter the historical prominence of the mulatto ruling elite, which through the army had manipulated the nation politically and economically for most of its history. For Duvalier, a black in a society dominated by people of lighter skin, power offered security beyond his boyhood wish for greater physical presence.

Duvalier's rise was as inauspicious as his manner and appearance. By November 1929, the shy 22-year-old medical student watched silently from the sidelines as resistance to the American occupation in Port-au-Prince hit its peak. Strikes and riots had become commonplace, and international condemnation of the American occupation forces followed. These events, combined with mounting economic problems in the United States, forced U.S. president Herbert Hoover to initiate a five-year plan for the withdrawal of the marine forces.

During the five-year withdrawal period Duvalier studied medicine and developed an intense interest in Voodoo, a word derived from the Fon language of West Africa meaning "spirit." Voodooists believe in one god, a result of French Catholic influence, but hold this god relatively distant, calling him "Le Grand Maître" (the Great Master). They maintain their African religious heritage by serving a pantheon of spirits, or *loa*, which have evolved into multiple expressions of "the Great Master." There are, for example, Erzulie, the erotic spirit of love, who is represented on Voodoo altars by pictures of the Virgin Mary; Damballah Ouedo, the snake spirit, who looks like St. Patrick; and Papa Legba, who, like St. Peter standing at heaven's gate, guards the entrance to Guinée, a sort of spirit heaven. Together these spirits and literally hundreds of others "spin a web of belief" that generates a sense of "total comprehension of the universe," as it was put by Wade Davis, a Harvard University botanist and cultural researcher who studied the religion while living among Haitian peasants during the 1980s.

Haitians are fond of saying that the Catholic goes to church to speak about god, whereas the Voodooist dances in the temple to become god. During a Voodoo ceremony the spirits are called upon to possess one or more of the congregants in order to advise them on how to achieve health, wealth, love, and happiness. During possessions, believers, in a frenzied dance, move into a deep hypnotic trance that allows them to perform seemingly superhuman feats such as eating fire or chewing glass. The spirits may be gentle or violent in their treatment of the possessed body, depending on which of two rituals is used: *rada* rites, which invoke benevolent spirits, or *petro* rites, which invoke malevolent spirits. One spirit may embody good or evil depending on which ritual is used; Erzulie, for instance, is beautiful and friendly when summoned through a rada rite but ugly and angry when called during a petro ceremony. François Duvalier would eventually exhibit rada and petro qualities in his own Dr. Jekyll/Mr. Hyde persona as a tool for manipulating his superstitious people.

> *Haiti is 80 percent Catholic,*
> *100 percent Voodoo.*
> —Old Haitian proverb

The village of Dondon in northeast Haiti. Belief in Voodoo was often the central element in the life of inhabitants of such isolated rural villages, home for the majority of the country's black population. The village *houngan*, or Voodoo priest, was often the most important individual in such communities.

For Duvalier, a Roman Catholic by birth, the study of Voodoo unlocked the mysteries and myths of Haiti and of the Haitian people. Voodoo has survived persecution in large part because it is geared to the Haitian peasants' harsh way of life. For generations, more than 85 percent of the population has lived in small, rural Voodoo communities called *combites*. According to Davis, each combite, which may be composed of several thatched-roof villages, has responsibility for planting and harvesting crops and maintaining the local Voodoo temple, or *honfour*, and Voodoo priest, or houngan. Because Voodoo prescribes not only a complex body of belief but also a set of laws that regulate social behavior, the houngan is the leader of his combite and the sole interpreter of the universe for his often isolated and illiterate congregation.

Duvalier discovered that from this isolation sprang a unique society based on Africanism: the value of collective labor, communal land holdings, the family, and the authority of the patriarchal figure or "Papa"; the importance of art, music, dance, and the oral transmission of songs and folklore; and the evolution of complex systems of justice and medicine. Duvalier's early interest in Voodoo may have been sparked by the houngans' knowledge of pain-killing narcotic plants and home remedies such as using salt to treat shock. Such was his expertise that in 1944 he would write a book, *The Gradual Evolution of Voodoo*, and be considered a full-fledged houngan in his own right.

Duvalier received his medical diploma in 1934, the year the last marines departed Haiti. But while Dr. Duvalier quietly interned at the Hospice Saint-François-de-Sales, the urban poor—tasting freedom for the first time in almost two decades—attempted to destroy all that reminded them of the American occupation. They tore up bridges, buildings, and irrigation lines just as their ancestors had done after Napoleon withdrew his forces in 1803. President Sténio Vincent—a mulatto who was elected to office by the elite during the five-year marine withdrawal—responded to the unrest by declaring martial law, suspending the constitution, and ousting opposition members of the congress. He thus became Haiti's first postoccupation dictator. Vincent's "presidency" signaled the resumption of politics-as-usual in Haiti.

As President Vincent settled into the gleaming white presidential palace, Duvalier began to take more of an interest in politics. He contributed articles to the daily newspaper *Action Nationale*, writing under the pen name Abderrahman (the French phonetic spelling of Abd-al-Rahman, the 10th-century Arab leader who founded the medical school of Córdoba, Spain). As Abderrahman, Duvalier criti-

A worshiper possessed by a spirit during a Voodoo ceremony. Haitian rural life is organized around Voodoo secret societies, which regulate religious, social, legal, and even commercial affairs. In the 1940s, Duvalier's work as a rural doctor earned him the full support of the secret societies.

cized the elite for their selfishness and their lack of interest in the masses, whose poverty "enraged" him. Always a quiet, extremely shy man, Duvalier assumed at times the fiery identity he had given to Abderrahman in his writings. This tendency to idealize greatness in himself by assuming the identity of past heroes gradually became an obsession.

Duvalier and his friend Lorimer Denis became founding members of a literary group named *Les Griots*, from a West African word meaning "poet" or "minstrel." The group's members embraced the African roots of the Haitian people and regarded Voodoo as a legitimate religion, the essential source of Haitian art, music, dance, and literature. In 1938 Les Griots began irregularly publishing a magazine, and within its pages the seed of the Duvalier movement was sown.

On December 27, 1939, Duvalier married Simone Ovide, a soft-spoken nurse and the illegitimate daughter of a Port-au-Prince merchant. She was mulatto, and Duvalier and many others in Haiti considered his marriage to her a step up the social ladder. Years later, in spite of his problack and antimulatto rhetoric, Duvalier would insist that his son and two of his three daughters also marry mulattoes.

Duvalier supported his family in the early 1940s by working for a joint Haitian-American aid project aimed at controlling the spread of yaws, a crippling disease that at the time affected 78 percent of the population. In 1943, Duvalier was named director of the new antiyaws training center in Gressier, a town located on the outskirts of Port-au-Prince. The Gressier clinic was popular; it grew from 25 patients a week to as many as 1,000 a day, putting Duvalier into direct contact with the peasants who came to the clinic from the surrounding countryside. Because good health was something mystically sacred to the peasants, whose short lives were riddled with disease and hardship, they came to regard Duvalier as a man endowed with the spiritual power to restore order in their bodies. Duvalier's knowledge of modern and folk medicine gave him a kind of super-houngan status.

As the battle against yaws expanded with the availability of penicillin — the real reason for Duvalier's success in curing the disease — so did his visibility. Mobile clinics were sent to mountain villages, where Duvalier and his assistants administered the drug to infected peasants. This venture allowed Duvalier to establish important relationships with the leaders of the Voodoo communities, impressing them with his healing abilities and his knowledge of their religion.

In August 1944, Duvalier was one of 20 Haitian doctors selected by a U.S. government commission to study tropical diseases at the University of Michigan. He spent two semesters there, then returned to Haiti to take part in a malaria-control program. At this point, Duvalier began referring to himself as "just a little country doctor" who treats "his children" — their "Papa Doc." By calling himself "Papa," Duvalier was appealing to the African sense of patriarchy so ingrained in the social structure of the Voodoo communities.

Duvalier came to believe what the peasants had already known for decades: that there were really two distinct Haitis — the Haiti of Port-au-Prince, with its French-based mulatto influences, and the black rural Haiti, with its roots in Africa. Duvalier recognized that the power base of Haiti's mulatto leaders lay in the elite of Port-au-Prince. He also saw that the best way for a black man to become president was by building a power base in the traditional Voodoo societies of the countryside.

While Duvalier battled yaws and malaria in rural Haiti, the urban blacks of Port-au-Prince — many of whom had adopted the customs and religion of the French — struggled for political, social, and economic acceptance by the mulatto elite. In 1946 the new class of urban blacks succeeded when one of their number rose to power after a series of coups. President Vincent had resigned unexpectedly, and his successor, also a mulatto, was quickly deposed after he was found to be an ally of General Rafael Trujillo, the dictator of the Dominican Republic. (Relations between Haiti and the Dominican Republic had been strained since 1937, when Trujillo's

Dumarsais Estimé, who became Haiti's president in 1946 and named a former student of his, François Duvalier, director of public health. Estimé's programs improved the economy, but he was overthrown by Paul Magloire in 1950. Duvalier vowed revenge upon Magloire and the mulatto elite that put him in power.

army massacred more than 20,000 Haitian cane cutters as they migrated across the border looking for work.) With the capital in a state of chaos following the coup, the elite-dominated Haitian congress decided to elevate a black political unknown to the presidency: Dumarsais Estimé, Duvalier's old secondary-school teacher.

Estimé immediately named his former student director of public health. Duvalier quickly advanced through the ranks and in 1949 was promoted to the president's cabinet as minister of health and labor. He moved his family to a middle-class neighborhood where, despite the increase in his salary, he continued to live modestly, not even owning a refrigerator.

Despite his rapid promotion, Duvalier accomplished little as a cabinet minister. He was described as secretive, arousing little enmity, making few strong impressions on anyone. Estimé, on the other hand, embarked on an aggressive campaign to improve Haiti's economy. He increased the minimum daily wage for workers from 30 to 75 cents, attempted to create Haiti's first social security system, improved the business climate by encouraging foreign investment, developed the tourist industry, instituted an income tax to pay for it all, and even required peasants to wear shoes in the capital city.

Yet the rift between black and mulatto widened. The urban blacks, long denied entry into Haiti's corrupt business community but newly empowered through their position in the Estimé government, simply enriched themselves by siphoning off public funds. Political scandals erupted like volcanoes.

The mulatto elite found an ally in Colonel Paul Magloire, a black strongman with an eye on the presidency. On May 10, 1950, Magloire deposed and exiled Estimé in a bloodless coup. A bitter Duvalier went back to his old job with the American medical service and began to plot Magloire's overthrow.

On October 8, 1950, Magloire won a six-year term as president in a fraudulent election. He improved on the economic base laid down by the pioneering Estimé by introducing a five-year plan for basic development and industrialization. The arts, encouraged under Estimé, flourished under Magloire. Port-

The people present the sad spectacle of black misery in the heart of riches. The nation has sufficient wealth, but it is not properly distributed. It is the wretched condition of the masses which drove Dr. Duvalier into politics to begin with.
—FRANÇOIS DUVALIER

au-Prince became a favorite haunt for artists, writers, and theater people from the United States and Great Britain, including Noel Coward, Truman Capote, Irving Berlin, and Graham Greene, who would one day write *The Comedians*, a novel critical of Haiti under Duvalier. Magloire basked in goodwill, becoming the first president in Haitian history to enjoy popularity with the outside world.

But the more Magloire's popularity increased, the more Duvalier seethed in anger and thought of revenge. On the surface Magloire had established a balance between color and classes, though in fact he favored the mulatto elite. The historic tension between men of light and dark skin arose once again, and Duvalier was quick to marshal his forces. He recruited Clément Barbot, a tall, sharp-featured black man. Barbot, a former teacher, was manipulative and intelligent; he possessed the skills that Duvalier needed and had no qualms about killing anyone who got in his way. Together they made a powerful and cunningly dangerous team.

Haitian president Paul Magloire (left) shakes hands with U.S. president Dwight Eisenhower during a 1955 visit to Washington, D.C. Magloire, though popular abroad for developing Haiti's economy, was forced out of office in 1956 by domestic unrest, in part fomented by Duvalier.

In 1954, Magloire, who had two years left in his term, took official notice of the movement against him. He sent word to the American medical service to fire Duvalier for using his post as a front for political activities. When Duvalier heard this he went into hiding and with Barbot's help staged student demonstrations, bombings, and strikes. Superstitious peasants refused to bring produce to the Port-au-Prince marketplace because Duvalier told them that *loups garous* (werewolves) were on the loose and would tear them apart if they tried to enter the city. Magloire's police reacted to the unrest by killing several students and arresting many others.

In August 1956, Duvalier came out of hiding after his men convinced Magloire that it was not the mild-mannered doctor who was behind the turmoil but other opposition candidates after the president's job. Less than a month later, on September 7, 1956, Duvalier formally announced his candidacy for the office of president in the upcoming elections. He began setting up campaign headquarters in Voodoo temples and urged the houngans to get out the vote. A few weeks after Duvalier announced his intentions, Lorimer Denis died. Rumors spread that Duvalier had offered his old friend's body to the Voodoo spirits in exchange for the presidency.

Magloire tried to cancel the upcoming elections, but the military had lost confidence in him and advised him to leave office — or else. He resigned on December 12, 1956, and flew to exile in Jamaica the following day. Haitians celebrated the beginning of a new era of democracy. Or so they thought.

During the next nine months the government of Haiti changed hands six times — two governments by executive council, three provisional presidents, and finally a group of military officers who formed a ruling junta. After several false starts the junta set the date of the election for September 22, 1957. Duvalier, meanwhile, had persuaded the military that his two black opponents in the presidential race were responsible for crimes against the state; one was expelled, and the other was driven into hiding.

It was now a two-man race between a black and a mulatto, just the way Duvalier wanted it. His opponent was Louis Déjoie, a 60-year-old Belgian-educated agricultural engineer and a member of the Port-au-Prince mulatto elite. Déjoie condemned the Négritude movement of the 1940s as a "decade of social regression" and proclaimed that his election to the presidency would mean a new era of industrial and business prosperity. Déjoie was supported by Haiti's Roman Catholic church, by the U.S. embassy, and by American business interests. But he antagonized the army by promising to thoroughly reorganize it — a move the army feared was aimed at weakening its political power.

So the military backed Duvalier, mistakenly believing that he would be an easily manipulated front man for a regime in which it would hold the real

François Duvalier brings his 1957 campaign for the presidency to the countryside. Styling himself as Papa Doc, the champion of the impoverished black majority, Duvalier set up headquarters in Voodoo temples and relied on the houngans to get out the vote. He won by more than a 2-to-1 margin.

Duvalier in battle garb during a July 1958 coup attempt led by Alix Pasquet, a former Haitian army officer. The failed coup convinced Duvalier of the need to eliminate all potential opposition and resulted in the formation of the Volunteers for National Security, popularly known as the Tontons Macoutes.

power. Some members of the mulatto elite supported Duvalier for the same reason, even though he advocated their removal from public office and from economic power. Duvalier did nothing during the campaign to discourage the two groups' impression of him.

For the first time in 153 years of independence, all Haitians 21 and older were allowed to vote. The problem was that Haiti had no voter-registration or birth-certification system; there was no way of telling who was eligible and who was not. The situation was chaotic on election day. A primitive system devised to prevent people from voting twice — the little finger on the voter's right hand was dipped in red ink and the fingernail clipped — failed miserably, and voter fraud was rampant. In the end, Duvalier beat Déjoie 679,884 votes to 266,993, and the Duvalierists won all the congressional seats from districts outside of Port-au-Prince. For the first time in the history of the republic, the rural provinces controlled the government.

On October 22, 1957, Duvalier was inaugurated president. Thereafter, 22 was the president's lucky number. He christened himself "Papa Doc" and set about removing those who had voted against him: the urban blacks, the mulattoes, and almost the entire business community in Port-au-Prince. Duvalier's newly appointed chief aide, Clément Barbot, did the dirty work.

Within weeks hundreds of Duvalier's political enemies were thrown in jail or simply disappeared. Whenever anyone was arrested, Barbot did the interrogating; prisoners either talked or died, sometimes both. Duvalier's crackdown sent hundreds of Haitians to the foreign embassies in Port-au-Prince seeking asylum and safe passage out of the country; one of them was Déjoie, who managed to escape to Cuba.

In addition, Duvalier forced many officers in the top command of Haiti's 5,000-man army to retire. This was meant to prevent any attempts by the military to overthrow him. But in July 1958 such an attempt materialized, and although it involved a force of only eight men, it almost succeeded.

The attempted coup was led by former Haitian army captain Alix Pasquet, an outspoken exile living in Miami who had supported Déjoie in the elections. Along with two other former army officers, he hired two deputies from Miami's Dade County and three other Americans to invade Haiti. The eight men sailed from the Florida Keys, landed in Haiti's Gulf of Gonâve, and forced a truck driver to take them to the army barracks located behind the National Palace. They surprised the sleeping soldiers inside and locked them in their quarters, then called the palace and ordered Duvalier to surrender. The rebels, Pasquet told Duvalier, controlled the barracks and the rest of the country.

Duvalier had packed his bags and was prepared to flee with his family to the Colombian embassy. But, incredibly, one of the invaders sent a captive out to buy a pack of cigarettes; the captive promptly walked over to the presidential palace and told Duvalier that the invasion force consisted of only eight men. Duvalier smiled, unpacked, and ordered his guards to go over to the barracks and kill them.

A barrage of machine-gun fire and a few hand-grenade explosions ended the assault. Hearing nothing, the government soldiers broke into the barracks and found that the invaders were all dead.

Over the next few days Duvalier, in steel helmet and army fatigues, wearing a .45-caliber pistol on his belt and carrying another in his pocket, triumphantly rode around Port-au-Prince. This was a side of the mild-mannered physician that the people had not yet seen — the Mr. Hyde to Papa Doc's Dr. Jekyll. Duvalier had defeated the invaders and had learned a very important lesson in the process: He needed a personal militia to stay in power.

Obsessed by his need for security, power, and control, Duvalier formed the 10,000-man Volunteers for National Security. The public called them the Tontons Macoutes, after a Creole folk tale in which a bogeyman posing as the uncle, or *tonton*, of misbehaving children carries them off in his knapsack, or *macoutes*, never to be seen again. It was an ominous sign for the people of Haiti: Papa Doc had become the latest Haitian strongman.

> *I am not a dictator. I consider myself a country doctor. I want to build up Haiti.*
> —FRANÇOIS DUVALIER

43

4

Voodoo, the Tool of Power

The Tontons Macoutes supplied the force that ensured François Duvalier's total control over Haiti. The fanatical loyalty of this nationwide network of security, intelligence, and terror was rewarded with an unwritten license to steal, torture, and kill. Often they would slit the throats of their victims and hang the bodies in the marketplace to rot in the hot sun as an example of what could happen to anti-Duvalierists.

From their formation in 1958 up until 1963, the Tontons Macoutes were indirectly funded, armed, and trained by the United States. At Duvalier's request, the United States reestablished a marine training mission in Haiti and began instructing Macoutes, who were disguised as regular members of the Haitian army. U.S. Marine colonel Robert Heinl, the head of the mission, became a frequent dinner guest of Clément Barbot, the powerful nationwide leader of the Tontons Macoutes and the man who had orchestrated Duvalier's rise to power. The psychological impact of the U.S. presence was not lost on Duvalier's opponents, who referred to the marines as white Tontons Macoutes.

[The Tontons Macoutes] has only one soul: Duvalier; recognizes only one chief: Duvalier; fights for only one destiny: Duvalier in power.
—FRANÇOIS DUVALIER

François Duvalier and his wife, Simone. During his first five years in power, Papa Doc dissolved the Haitian legislature, outlawed political parties and labor unions, attacked the power of the Roman Catholic church, and ordered the Tontons Macoutes to arrest and torture hundreds of alleged dissidents.

Duvalier chats with U.S. Marine colonel Robert Heinl at the National Palace in February 1959. Heinl headed the U.S. mission charged with training the Haitian military. The marine advisers also trained the newly formed Tontons Macoutes.

Duvalier was able to establish the Tontons Macoutes with great speed because of his knowledge of and connection with Haiti's Voodoo secret societies. Papa Doc not only recruited rural secret society leaders for government posts, he also used their underground network as the structural basis for his Macoutes. This led to what has been called "the Voodooization of Haitian politics" under Duvalier.

The secret societies of the Haitian countryside were the unofficial governing authority of the rural masses. The societies comprised elaborate underground religious and judicial bodies, paramilitary forces, and spies, whose function was to protect not only Voodoo and its practitioners but in some cases Duvalierism as well. Over the years Duvalier's enemies would mount several guerrilla campaigns and coup attemps, but all failed, in large part because they underestimated the strength of the ties between the president, the secret societies, and the Creole-speaking masses.

The roots of the secret societies run deep into Haiti's past. Escaped slaves, called *Maroons*, formed clandestine organizations in the mountainous regions of Haiti to protect themselves from discovery by French plantation owners. The Maroons created secret armed camps, cleared forests to plant food, and supplemented what they grew by raiding plantations. Acceptance into the ranks of the Maroons was strictly controlled. New arrivals were subjected to a rigorous initiation, during which they were tested for endurance and pain and were taught the secret passwords and handshakes that would distinguish friend from foe during attacks on plantations. Slaves captured during raids were sometimes forced to work on the Maroon farms, and at the slightest suggestion of betrayal they were put to death.

The military tactics of the Maroons — raids, fire, poison, ambush — and their secret communications network contributed substantially to the slaves' victory over Napoleon's armies during the Haitian Revolution. But although the Maroons played an important role in the war for independence, the first black leaders of the republic, Dessalines and Christophe, feared them and tried to annihilate them. They failed, and ever since then, the descendants of the Maroons distrusted whoever held power at the National Palace. While monarchies and dictatorships came and went in Port-au-Prince — each followed by anarchy and then by the restoration of despotic order — the underground authority of the communities lived on, virtually uninterrupted. Behind the veil of secrecy that allowed them to survive, these Maroon communities developed political, economic, and religious systems of their own, eventually evolving into the secret societies of present-day Haiti.

Duvalier understood the historic division between the French-inspired government and culture of Port-au-Prince and the secret societies of the masses, and he sought to erase the lines between them. He incorporated the societies into the national government by recruiting their leaders as lo-

Voodoo poison makers exhibit the tools of their trade in a photo taken by Harvard cultural researcher Wade Davis, who lived among the secret societies of rural Haiti. Duvalier appointed society leaders to head local units of the Tontons Macoutes, thus extending his hold throughout rural Haiti.

cal and regional Tontons Macoutes bosses. This provided the thread that stitched together the disparate cultures of Port-au-Prince and the countryside all under one commander in chief. Duvalier ran his government like the armed camps of the Voodoo secret societies, alternately breeding fear and inspiring devotion among the people.

Many of Duvalier's top officials were members of the *Bizango*, an ancient West African tribal name for what is believed to be Haiti's largest secret society. Little was known about the Bizango until it was penetrated in 1984 by the Harvard University botanist and cultural researcher Wade Davis, who, building on the groundwork laid by the anthropologists Zora Neale Hurston and Michel Laguerre, shed some light on the secret culture. Davis discovered that the altars of Bizango temples were decorated with pictures of Duvalier, who he believes may have become the "symbolic or effective head" of the society. In addition, the flag of the Bizango, whose motto is Order and Respect for the Night, was represented by the colors of blood and night. Duvalier would eventually use these colors — red and black—to create a new national flag for Haiti.

The power structure of the Bizango reflected the influences of the French court, American democracy, and African tribal patriarchy. There were emperors and queens, presidents and secretaries, and *bokors* (sorcerers), houngans, *mambos* (Voodoo priestesses), *malfactuers* (evildoers), and *hounsis* (members).

Under Duvalier, membership in the Bizango — open to men and women by invitation and initiation — could virtually secure survival. The Bizango, it is said, can be "sweet as honey or bitter as bile." Members accused of infractions were brought before a council of elders during meetings, called *séances*, held after dark. The séances were ritualistic as well as business related. They could include long processions to a cemetery, where the spirit of one of the society's most important gods, the Baron Samedi, was invoked and the blood of a sacrificial animal was drunk by the members.

It was within this powerful context that the elders, acting as judge and jury, decided on punishment, which could mean exile, death, or "zombification," the displacement of the soul. As Davis points out, many powerful Macoutes acted as bokors, who could create a zombie by causing an unnatural magical "death" — the act of zombification. In many cases the bokor accomplished this by administering a topically active poison to the condemned. The poison induces a paralytic state that mimics death by suppressing the body's metabolic rate to the point where a victim might live for hours on the amount of oxygen trapped in a coffin. The victim would be declared dead, be buried, and then be exhumed by the bokor at night to become his "slave" (if the zombie is not exhumed in time the victim suffers brain damage or dies from lack of oxygen).

With the Bizango and other secret societies performing rituals in Duvalier's name, the peasants soon believed that he himself possessed magical powers. Duvalier encouraged that belief by affecting not only the appearance but the personality of the Baron Samedi, the lord of the cemetery and of zombies, represented in Voodoo rites by the cross of

> *For the sick, or the troubled, [Bizango] is a wonderful thing, whether you have money or not. But it is only good because it can be very bad. If you get into trouble with it, it can be very hard on you.*
> —JEAN BAPTISTE
> emperor of a Bizango
> secret society

Jesus Christ. Duvalier had always dressed in black suits and white shirts — the Baron's traditional garb — but after the 1958 invasion by Alix Pasquet, his face began to take on an otherworldly sheen, as if he had applied some kind of oil. When addressing the public he would be alternately explosive, at times using an unintelligible mixture of French and Creole, and passive, speaking in a whisper, drooping his eyelids, wearing a bemused half-smile, and doing nothing for long periods of time. The peasants were awed.

Thus, by mixing belief in the supernatural with government and military force, Duvalier successfully created a police state capable of supervising and controlling the actions of its citizens at every level.

Beyond the scope of the supernatural, Duvalier needed the U.S. government to train and supply the Tontons Macoutes. And he got it, thanks to developments in nearby Cuba. In December 1958 a young, educated, and charismatic Cuban named Fidel Castro had surprised the world by staging a successful revolution and ousting Fulgencio Batista, Cuba's corrupt dictator. Upon assuming power,

Flanked by soldiers and Macoutes, Duvalier addresses the Haitian people from the steps of the National Palace on May 22, 1963, the last day of the "Month of Gratitude," during which he ordered public officials to give speeches extolling his virtues. Papa Doc's behavior grew increasingly erratic as time wore on.

Castro promised to come to the aid of all revolutionary groups who wished to overthrow repressive regimes in their homelands. Because many of those regimes sheltered lucrative American business enterprises, the U.S. government kept a watchful eye on Castro. When Duvalier promised to oppose Castro, the U.S. Marine base in Haiti became a training center for the Haitian military — and the Tontons Macoutes.

While Haitian exiles flocked to Castro's side and fueled rumors of a pending Cuban invasion of Haiti, Duvalier suffered a massive heart attack complicated by diabetes. On May 24, 1959, he very nearly died. As doctors worked to ensure his recovery over the ensuing weeks, Clément Barbot, whose skill in eliminating the regime's enemies had earned him the nickname "Muffler," effectively ran the government.

On August 30, 1959, a 30-man Cuban invasion force landed in Haiti. With his customary efficiency, Barbot had his Macoutes wipe out the invaders within four days, killing more peasants than Cubans in the process; those peasants who collaborated, even only slightly, were exterminated. Castro claimed he knew nothing about the invasion. Barbot, meanwhile, reveled in the glory of his success —and that turned out to be a grave mistake.

Duvalier began to suspect Barbot of trying to undermine his control and seize the presidency. Power struggles among the regional leaders of the Tontons Macoutes erupted and fed Duvalier's suspicions that a coup was being planned. On July 14, 1960, Duvalier's Presidential Guard arrested Barbot on trumped-up charges of treason. Barbot, pretending to be a born-again Christian repentant for his evil deeds, was released from jail 16 months later, bent on revenge.

With Barbot temporarily out of the way, further developments in Cuba had given Duvalier more leverage in his effort to gain aid money from the United States. Cuba was the main supplier of sugar to the United States, so when Castro vowed to end U.S. dominance over the Cuban economy and took over the island's sugar plantations, the American

Fidel Castro, leader of the revolution that overthrew Cuban dictator Fulgencio Batista in 1958. The United States, wary of Castro's vow to help others oust dictators throughout the Caribbean, stepped up aid to the dictators it supported. Duvalier was one who benefited greatly from increased U.S. aid.

After crushing virtually all opposition within Haiti, Papa Doc (center) had himself inaugurated president-for-life in June 1964. "I am a giant capable of eclipsing the sun," Duvalier told his listeners that day.

government was angered; suspecting that Castro was a communist, the U.S. Central Intelligence Agency (CIA) directed Florida-based anti-Castro exiles in a secret war against Cuba. Duvalier, meanwhile, had already gained from the U.S. effort against Castro when the United States bought Haitian sugar to replace what it had been buying from Cuba.

But the real bonanza for Duvalier came in 1961, with the complete failure of a CIA-directed invasion of Cuba that became known as the Bay of Pigs affair. With the defeat of the invasion force, made up of Cuban exiles, Castro declared that he was a communist and began to strengthen ties with the Soviet Union. Duvalier announced that he was an opponent of communism, and the grateful Americans responded by stepping up aid to Haiti. By 1962, Duvalier's government had received more than $50 million in direct U.S. economic and military aid — more than half of which was used to support the Tontons Macoutes and the Presidential Guard.

In the early 1960s Duvalier used his overwhelming power to crush all opposition. After pro-Castro students declared a massive strike against the schools, Duvalier declared martial law, outlawed all youth organizations — including the Boy Scouts — and purged the faculties of all suspected opponents. Thereafter, only the children of the Tontons Macoutes or others in government favor received priority for admission and scholarships.

Duvalier also moved against his opponents in the Roman Catholic church. He charged Monsignor François Poirier, a leading church official, with giving communist students money to overthrow the government and expelled him from the country. Poirier was flown to Miami in his white cassock with only a book and one dollar in his pocket — a symbol of the price at which Duvalier valued the monsignor's life. Other priests would follow into exile for, among other things, refusing to include the president in their prayers. The Vatican replied to the expulsions by excommunicating Papa Doc, who, after getting rid of the priests, began referring to himself as "the spiritual leader of the country." Duvalier had Zachary Delva, one of his regional Macoutes chiefs and a powerful Bizango leader, conduct a Voodoo ceremony on the steps of the Gonaïves Cathedral. Delva invited the public and officiated in the rites, which included the sacrifice of pigs as blood offerings to the Voodoo spirits.

Appalled by Duvalier's brutality, U.S. president John F. Kennedy attempted to cut off aid to Haiti. But Duvalier responded by threatening to withdraw his support for U.S. positions in international organizations. In January 1962 the Organization of American States (OAS, an association of all the independent nations of the Western Hemisphere) met in Uruguay and, bowing to American pressure, expelled Cuba as a member. Duvalier told the U.S. delegation he would cast his ballot against American policies unless the United States paid the Haitian government at least $7.25 million. The Americans complied. Duvalier tried the tactic again at other OAS meetings and at the United Nations, but finally, in May 1963, a disgusted Kennedy halted all military aid. By then it was too late; Duvalier was firmly entrenched as Haiti's absolute dictator.

In April 1961, Duvalier called for an election, even though he still had more than two years to go on his original six-year term. He dissolved both houses of the congress and replaced them with a single 58-member assembly. Fifty-eight candidates, all supporters of the president, were nominated, and the people were called to the polls. With only one name

He knows Haitians better than Haitians know themselves. He knows what they're thinking before they think it. And because of this he is always one jump ahead of everyone else. The first error in judgement Papa Doc makes will be his last—and he knows it. This man is as shrewd—and as evil—as Hitler was.
—a foreign businessman's description of Duvalier

Rafael Trujillo, dictator of the Dominican Republic from 1930 to 1961. In 1937, Trujillo's army massacred 20,000 Haitian migrant workers, yet he enjoyed close relations with several Haitian leaders, including Duvalier. His assassination in May 1961 increased Papa Doc's paranoia and brought a new round of Macoutes repression.

on the ballot, "Dr. François Duvalier, president," there was no way of voting against the list. Five days later the government announced that Duvalier had been "reelected" with 1.3 million votes.

Duvalier's inauguration on May 22, 1961, was cheered by more than 200,000 Haitian peasants carrying the Voodoo flags representing their respective societies. The peasants had been transported from the mountains to the capital by Duvalier's troops for three days of free food and rum. During his acceptance speech the 54-year-old president pledged to promote "true democracy" and to provide an example of liberty for his "African brothers."

A week later Duvalier's exaltation came to an end when the Dominican dictator Trujillo was assassinated by seemingly loyal army officers. After Trujillo's death, Papa Doc became truly paranoid: He now believed that everyone was untrustworthy and out to get him. Duvalier ordered the Tontons Macoutes to kill anyone who was even remotely a threat to the regime, and his oft-quoted justification, "We don't kill people, only enemies," was little comfort to those around him. Cabinet officials, assemblymen, and military officers, upon learning that they were out of favor, immediately sought asylum at the foreign embassies in Port-au-Prince. The embassies overflowed with exiles. Those who managed to get out of the country joined other Haitian exiles throughout the Caribbean who were plotting Duvalier's ouster.

His sense of grandeur and omnipotence became more pronounced. In July 1961, Duvalier announced the construction of a model city as a monument to himself. For its site he chose a village 20 miles north of Port-au-Prince named Cabaret, which would be renamed Duvalierville. To finance the project, Papa Doc levied heavy taxes on such vital foods as sugar, rice, and edible oils. He forced government workers to contribute 10 percent of their monthly salaries and instructed the Macoutes to shake down foreign businessmen for "contributions" to the National Renovation Movement, a fund-raising organization headed by Luckner Cambronne, a young student who rose to prominence with such pronouncements as

> a good Duvalierist should be ready to kill his children, and good Duvalierist children should be ready to kill their parents for the sake of Duvalierism.

Now the Macoutes were in full swing. As the rewards of the system became evident, membership in the Macoutes became very loosely defined. Nearly all government employees belonged and were subject to off-duty calls. Some received a monthly stipend of $30 to $50; others operated for the prestige and the unwritten license to swagger, steal, and murder. As their wealth grew the Macoutes began taking on a more gangsterlike appearance, wearing dark glasses and fedoras.

Events in Haiti grew increasingly bizarre. In April 1963 a group of predominantly mulatto Haitian exiles, this time operating out of the Dominican Republic, announced that it would invade Haiti and overthrow Duvalier. The group's leaflets said that a "dry-cleaning operation" would be carried out against "all noxious insects who accompany the gorilla," the gorilla presumably being Papa Doc. Duvalier responded to the leaflets by declaring a "Month of Gratitude," during which he was to be publicly exalted. From April 22 to May 22, the second anniversary of his inauguration for a second

Duvalier (dark suit) eyes Clément Barbot (foreground), the ruthless head of the Macoutes, in 1960. In the 1950s, Barbot loyally engineered Papa Doc's rise to power, but a few weeks after this photo was taken Duvalier jailed him for 16 months. After his release, Barbot led a rebellion against Duvalier in 1963.

Two Macoutes demonstrate their prowess with machetes at a celebration held during the Month of Gratitude. Paid only nominal salaries, the Tontons Macoutes survived on what they could extort or steal from the Haitian populace. After Barbot was killed and his revolt crushed, the Macoutes remained loyal to Papa Doc.

term, politicians, businessmen, and military figures were called upon to deliver speeches praising the president's regime. Refusal meant death. The Month of Gratitude was just one more of Duvalier's crafty power plays: At a critical time officials had to place themselves on record as Duvalierists, which meant that they would have to fight for their own lives as well as for Duvalier's in the event of a revolution.

The theme of the Month of Gratitude was sounded by Duvalier's personal physician, Dr. Jacques Foucard, the pistol-packing president of the Haitian Red Cross. At the official opening ceremony Foucard declared that a revolution would result in the greatest slaughter in history, producing "a Himalaya of corpses." He warned:

> Blood will flow in Haiti. The land will burn from north to south, from east to west; there will be no sunrise or sunset — just one big flame licking the sky. The dead will be buried under a mountain of ashes because of slavery to the foreigner.

The "foreigner" was, of course, the United States, which Foucard called "a democracy of sluts." His criticism was probably a reaction to President Kennedy's discontinuation of all nonhumanitarian aid to Haiti after May 15. (U.S. taxpayers had been directly subsidizing half of Haiti's $28.8 million annual budget.)

At this point Clément Barbot reentered the picture. Barbot sent word to the exile groups that he had a plan to topple Papa Doc. His scheme was to kidnap two of the Duvaliers' three children, who would then be exchanged for the president's resignation. And, incredibly enough, Barbot himself was to be the kidnapper.

On the morning of April 26, 1963, as Duvalier's limousine delivered the children to school, Barbot opened fire. He shot and killed the chauffeur and two bodyguards, while the children — 14-year-old Jean-Claude and 16-year-old Simone — scrambled into the school building unhurt. The abduction attempt botched, Barbot fled.

Duvalier's revenge was swift and ruthless. He ordered the Macoutes to round up all former military officers, their families, and their friends. At least 6 people were killed within 24 hours, executed summarily by the Macoutes merely on suspicion of being anti-Duvalierist. More than 100 others were arrested, half of whom were never seen again.

Duvalier, meanwhile, offered a $10,000 reward for Barbot's head. Undaunted, Barbot began to move more openly. He and his small group of followers raided arsenals and killed Macoutes. With every daring deed his legend grew. When a group of Macoutes stumbled upon the Barbot stronghold in the countryside, they surrounded the house and, thinking that Barbot was inside, riddled it with machine-gun fire. When they were done they kicked down the door, and an old black dog scampered out and ran into the bush. Acting on the Voodoo belief that the shadowy Barbot could change himself into a black dog, Duvalier ordered all black dogs shot.

On July 14, 1963, Barbot and a dozen followers were ready to try again. This time they would sneak into the palace and kill Duvalier. Exile groups based in the Dominican Republic would then invade Haiti and stage a revolution. But on the morning of the planned attack a peasant revealed Barbot's hideout in a village three miles north of Port-au-Prince. Duvalier's men moved in, trapped Barbot and his men in a field of sugarcane, and killed all of them. Papa Doc's most dangerous enemy was out of the way for good.

> *Duvalier is a mad man.*
> —CLÉMENT BARBOT
> at one time Duvalier's
> chief aide

5

President-for-Life

$\mathbf{F}$rail from heart disease and diabetes, Duvalier retreated deeper and deeper into Voodoo mysticism in his final years. Rumor had him studying goat entrails for guidance and communicating with the severed heads of his enemies. Yet despite his declining health and ever-increasing paranoia, Duvalier remained firmly in control and paved the way for Jean-Claude's ascent to power.

The Barbot rebellion and Duvalier's bloody reaction to it rekindled the historical hatred between Haiti and the Dominican Republic. While Barbot was still at large the Macoutes, instead of limiting their usual antics to Haitians, got carried away and slashed the throat of a member of the Dominican diplomatic corps. As tensions mounted, Duvalier ordered his army to burn a three-mile swath along the entire length of the border to keep Haitians in and any further exile invasions out.

In April 1963 the two countries moved to the brink of war when Duvalier insisted that some of Barbot's men were taking refuge in the Dominican embassy near Port-au-Prince and ordered his troops to rout them out. Duvalier's guards stormed the embassy, searched the ground floor, and questioned diplomatic personnel at rifle point. Upon

> *Duvalier may be a megalomaniac, but don't underestimate him. He is the master of psychology.*
> —Anonymous U.S. state department official

Duvalier with members of the Presidential Guard at a state function in 1963. With Barbot out of the way, Papa Doc's authority went unquestioned. He deliberately fostered the impression among Haitian peasants that he was an incarnation of Baron Samedi, the Voodoo lord of the cemetery.

U.S. president John F. Kennedy (right) with Dominican president Juan Bosch in 1963. After years of U.S. aid to Haiti — mainly to finance the Macoutes and the army — Kennedy cut off funding, partly in response to a crisis in which Duvalier ordered his men to lay siege to the Dominican embassy in Port-au-Prince.

hearing that all 22 of the men they were seeking were living temporarily at the Dominican ambassador's residence, Duvalier's guards surrounded the house and, in effect, held its occupants hostage.

Dominican president Juan Bosch, in office barely two months, quickly responded with a radio broadcast issuing Duvalier an ultimatum: "These outrages must end now. If they do not end within 24 hours we will end them." Bosch promised to bomb the presidential palace if Duvalier did not heed the warning and pull back his troops from the embassy residence. Responding in a long cable to Bosch, Duvalier vowed to defend himself by "all means available" in the event of an attack and accused the Dominicans of arming the invading Haitian exiles. Bosch denied the charge. "Duvalier is not only a dictator, he is a madman. There is no control over him. . . . I hope the Haitians get the job done as the Dominicans did," said Bosch, referring to the 1961 assassination of Trujillo.

The OAS, alarmed by the events on Hispaniola, called an emergency meeting in Washington and urged both Bosch and Duvalier to hold their fire until its investigating committee arrived in Port-au-Prince to look into the grievances. Both leaders agreed. Duvalier wanted to impress the OAS committee by creating a festive atmosphere for their arrival. He buried the decomposing bodies of the latest purge victims and declared an out-of-season Mardi Gras. Peasants were trucked into Port-au-Prince by the thousands. Free rum passed liberally through the crowds, who danced to the beat of drums while partisans chanted, "Duvalier or death! Duvalier or death!" As the tension mounted Bosch stationed 4,000 troops along the border, the British sent a Royal Navy frigate to evacuate personnel in the event of war, and the White House ordered a U.S. naval task force to patrol Haiti's coastline.

When OAS investigators arrived at the National Palace on April 30, they were immediately rebuffed by the Haitian president. Duvalier sat silently staring at each committee member for what was described by one investigator as an "embarrassingly long period of time" before finally acknowledging them with a nod of his head. Nothing more was said or done until that afternoon, when a crowd of 20,000 excited Haitians gathered outside the National Palace to hear the president's speech. Dressed like the Baron Samedi, Duvalier appeared on the balcony, raised his hands victoriously over his head, and delivered a garbled speech in both French and Creole: "I am the personification of the Haitian fatherland. Those who wish to destroy Duvalier wish to destroy the fatherland. . . . Duvalier is firm and unshakable. I ask you, Haitian people, to raise your souls to the height of the spirit of your ancestors, and to prove that you are men. . . . No foreigner is going to tell me what to do." Yet after the tough-sounding speech, Duvalier diplomatically agreed to pull back his troops and issue 15 passports to Dominicans for safe passage out of the country.

The OAS investigators packed up and left, and the British frigate and U.S. naval task force returned to their ports. Soon thereafter, in events that had nothing to do with Duvalier, the White House recalled its ambassador to Haiti (a man whom Papa Doc hated), Bosch was overthrown by the Dominican military, and Kennedy was assassinated. Papa Doc informed his Tontons Macoutes that Bosch,

> *[In] Haiti we have . . . democracy, Haitian democracy. And the man you call Papa Doc—in fact he is not a dictator, he is a democrat and his own people in this country consider him as a democrat because he is the leader of this nation.*
> —FRANÇOIS DUVALIER

Kennedy, and the U.S. ambassador to Haiti were gone due to his mystic will. The superstitious peasants, repeatedly subjected to Duvalier's Voodoo manipulations, believed that only a *gros nég*, a person protected by the gods, could wield so much power.

With Duvalier's successes, the government-controlled media began a new campaign of adulation, literally demanding that Duvalier become "president-for-life." The March 4, 1964, edition of *Le Journal d'Haïti* proclaimed:

> Duvalier is the professor of energy. Like Napoleon Bonaparte, Duvalier is the electrifier of souls, a powerful multiplier of energy. . . . Duvalier is one of the greatest leaders of contemporary times . . . because the renovator of the Haitian fatherland synthesizes all there is of courage, bravery, genius, diplomacy, patriotism, and tact in the titans of ancient and modern times.

> *All the people are terrorized. Duvalier is not sane. To remain in power, that's all he wants.*
> —FATHER JEAN-BAPTISTE
> GEORGES
> a Catholic priest and
> former friend of
> François Duvalier

The "voting," for lack of a better term, began at 6:00 A.M. on June 14. The ballots had all been marked yes in advance, and anyone caught writing in a no vote was arrested and charged with defacing the ballot. By 11:00 A.M. Duvalier, who had described himself as "this giant capable of eclipsing the sun because the people have consecrated me for life," appeared on the balcony of the presidential palace to deliver his acceptance speech. "Dr. Duvalier," he said, as usual referring to himself in the third person, "is a very distrustful man. He wants to lead as a master. He wants to lead as a true autocrat. That is to say, I repeat, he does not accept anyone before him but his own person. I'll rule with the firmness necessary."

Duvalier was inaugurated eight days later, on June 22, 1964. After reviewing a military parade and hearing speeches made in his honor, Papa Doc delivered a typically bizarre address to the crowd, including such assertions as:

> I never permit myself to be intoxicated. I remain equal to myself. While I listen to speeches, I talk to myself.

Three days of celebration followed.

Most Haitians had no idea that they had just approved a new 201-article constitution, which, besides granting Duvalier the presidency for life and absolute powers, referred to him as "the sovereign" — no coincidence, because Papa Doc was mulling the idea of proclaiming himself Emperor François I. But in the end he settled for the titles granted him by the new constitution: Supreme Chief of the Haitian Nation, Uncontestable Leader of the Revolution, Apostle of National Unity, Renovator of the Fatherland, Worthy Heir of the Founders of the Haitian Nation, Incorruptible Leader of the Great Majority of the Haitian People, and Spiritual Father of the Nation. These, however, did not compare with the self-flattery he wrote in one booklet, *The Catechism of the Revolution*, which contained Papa Doc's version of the Lord's Prayer:

> Our Doc who art in thy National Palace for life, hallowed be Thy name by present and future generations. Thy will be done at Port-au-Prince and in the provinces. Give us this day our new Haiti and never forgive the trespasses of the antipatriots who spit every day on our country; let them succumb to temptation, and under the weight of their venom, deliver them not from evil.

Jean-Claude (who was nearly kidnapped by Barbot during the 1963 revolt) and Nicole Duvalier, two of Papa Doc's four children, at the 1964 president-for-life inauguration ceremony. In the late 1960s, Papa Doc arranged for Jean-Claude to succeed him as president-for-life.

The booklet also substituted for the Roman Catholic explanation of the Holy Trinity a Papa Doc version:

"Q: Who are Dessalines, Toussaint, Christophe, Pétion, and Estimé?

"A: *Dessalines, Toussaint, Christophe, Pétion, and Estimé are five founders of the Haitian nation who are found within François Duvalier.*

"Q: Is Dessalines for life?

"A: *Yes, Dessalines is for life in François Duvalier.*"

The questions and answers were repeated for each of the four remaining founders and ended:

"Q: Do we conclude then that there are six presidents-for-life?

"A: *No, Dessalines, Toussaint, Christophe, Pétion, and Estimé are five distinct chiefs of state but who form only one and the same President in François Duvalier.*"

As lunatic as Papa Doc's version of the Holy Trinity may seem to some, it made sense to Voodooists, who believe that a man inherits the spirits of his ancestors. Duvalier promoted the idea that he was the composite of all the great revolutionary leaders of Haiti's past — something he had longed for since childhood. Although he declared himself a "Bible lover," Papa Doc claimed his true god was the "Africa Maître" and that the Voodoo spirits had made it possible for him to "ascend and assault." Duvalier further appealed to his compatriots in terms of their religion by adopting a new national flag using the red and black colors of the Bizango. "No standard can better express the joy of the nation of finding again in the strong mystique, the faith of its ancestors," he said.

A renewed series of small-scale exile invasions was under way in the second half of 1964. One group of 25, trained in secret in the Dominican Republic, was called the *Camoquins*, named after the antimalaria pill used in Haiti; they said they were the cure to the disease that was killing their country: Duvalierism. New recruits were called "aspirins" and were put through rigorous initiations.

Five days after Papa Doc's inauguration the Cam-

We can disregard any suggestion that Duvalier will leave office voluntarily. I think his ending will be apocalyptic; I think he will leave the National Palace feet first.
—ROBERT HEINL
retired U.S. Marine colonel

oquins launched their invasion from the Dominican Republic by boat, landing on Haiti's western shore on June 29, 1964. For several weeks they harassed Duvalier's troops as a hit-and-run force stationed in the rugged La Selle mountains. Duvalier, whose rural Macoutes chiefs in the combites informed him of the Camoquins' whereabouts, began making systematic arrests. All relatives of exiles and suspected anti-Duvalierists were jailed and beaten, and their businesses nationalized.

By mid-August the Camoquins were doomed to failure. The La Selle mountains had been almost completely denuded by frequent hurricanes, erosion, and peasant agricultural practices. There was no tree cover, no water, and no food. Cold, sick, and starving, the survivors retreated back across the border to the Dominican Republic.

Another group called *Jeune Haïti* (Young Haiti), 13 American-educated men, mostly mulattoes, timed their invasion to coincide with that of the Camoquins. Jeune Haïti had received CIA support and 30 days of guerrilla warfare training at the U.S.

In the late 1960s, Papa Doc immortalized his thoughts by writing several books, which featured the same disconnected style that marked his speeches. Suffering from heart disease and diabetes, Duvalier rarely left the National Palace in his later years.

Green Beret camp in North Carolina. On August 5 the Jeune Haïti guerrillas landed from the sea on the tip of the southwest peninsula and eluded government troops for the next 11 weeks. But they had completely underestimated Duvalier's political ties to the peasants. Tracked down, they fought to the last man before being wiped out. To prove they were dead, the government-controlled press furnished grisly photos of the dead Jeune Haïti guerrillas, including four severed heads held by anonymous hands against a white backdrop.

By this point Duvalier's paranoia had reached a stage at which he suspected his own family of plotting against him. His second daughter, Nicole, had married Luc Albert Foucard, a mulatto and the brother of Papa Doc's personal physician. His eldest and favorite daughter, Marie-Denise, had married a black palace guard, Colonel Max Dominique, whom Duvalier hated. He had wanted Marie-Denise to marry a mulatto, as he and Nicole had done.

The trouble began in April 1967, when two bombs exploded during Papa Doc's 60th-birthday celebration. Duvalier immediately suspected that Dominique was trying to embarrass Foucard, who had organized the event. He ordered 19 of Dominique's best friends to be rounded up, including some powerful Tontons Macoutes leaders from Dominique's hometown of Cap-Haïtien. All were loyal Duvalierists, but at Papa Doc's personal command they were tied to stakes and shot. One of the victims was Major Harry Tassy, the boyfriend of his 21-year-old daughter Simone.

Colonel Dominique did not appear at the reviewing stand during the annual June 22 festivities commemorating Duvalier's inauguration as president-for-life. With a theatrical flourish Papa Doc delivered his annual speech to more than 100,000 peasants, who had been trucked in for the occasion. "Duvalier is going to do something. He is going to make a roll call." He paused for effect. "Here is my call: Major Harry Tassy, where are you? Come to your benefactor. . . . Absent." In this way he called out the names of all 19 executed officers, then smiled and said, "They've all been shot." Of the 108

I'll rule with all the firmness necessary.
—FRANÇOIS DUVALIER

people who scrambled into foreign embassies in the wake of the executions, Duvalier flatly stated, "They are no longer Haitians," and had his assembly pass a resolution renouncing the international convention honoring political asylum. Colonel Dominique, Marie-Denise, and Simone were exiled at gunpoint the next day. The two women left with as much cash and jewelry as they could carry.

Twelve months would pass before Papa Doc allowed his children to return to Haiti, but when he did he seemed to have forgiven Marie-Denise. Considered the most intelligent of the Duvalier children, she became her father's personal secretary — one of the most powerful political positions in government. Duvalier pardoned her husband, Dominique, but forced him to remain in Paris as Haiti's ambassador to France. He also ordered Nicole to divorce Foucard, who had fallen out of favor. Other members of the family retreated from positions of power within the government, at least for the time being.

A market scene on a Port-au-Prince thoroughfare in 1969. Papa Doc's rule had lowered the average Haitian's already low income. Some believe that he spent part of his final years planning new economic programs for his son to implement when he took office.

The great Brazilian soccer star Pele pins a medal on Papa Doc in February 1971 while Jean-Claude and a presidential guardsman look on. This was François Duvalier's last public appearance. He died of a heart attack on April 21, 1971, having ruled Haiti for 14 years.

From 1968 until 1971, Duvalier is believed to have suffered at least one heart attack a year, each one complicated by the effects of diabetes. Although the government-controlled press did not mention Duvalier's declining health, rumors of power struggles within the government ran wild through the closed community of Port-au-Prince.

Duvalier's poor health and growing sense of mortality led to the publication of his collected works: *Thoughts*, a pocket-sized booklet answering questions in the manner of China's Mao Zedong; *The Essential Works of Duvalier*, a conglomeration of speeches; *Forty Years of Doctrine — Ten Years of Revolution — Breviary of a Revolution*, a compendium of articles and books from the late 1920s and 1930s; and *Memoirs of a Third World Leader*. All government workers who refused to buy the books were charged with being anti-Duvalierist. Duvalier made thousands of dollars on the sales.

Duvalier, now rarely seen in public, was rumored to be holed up in the National Palace working on a plan to improve Haiti's economy. A plan did eventually emerge, but too late to be of much help; the

Duvalier regime had already done enough damage. There was one doctor for every 10,000 Haitians, life expectancy was less than 33 years, the average per capita income had dropped from $75 to $65 a year, and the illiteracy rate was the same as it had been before the revolution of 1804. Tourism, a major source of income during the Magloire years, was nonexistent due to the savagery of Papa Doc's regime and the threat of war with the Dominican Republic. Hurricanes Flora (1963), Cleo (1964), and Inez (1966), each of which claimed scores of lives, wiped out crops and caused increased soil erosion. As if these problems were not enough, Duvalier's paranoia, coupled with the desperate economic situation, had forced the educated few to leave the country; for example, there were more Haitian doctors in Canada than there were in Haiti.

It was time, Duvalier said, for the young people to take over. In his Independence Day speech on January 1, 1971, Duvalier noted that Caesar Augustus was only 19 when he inherited the Roman Empire. "I will give power to youth when the time comes," he said, "because the future belongs to youth." By "youth" Duvalier meant his luxury-loving 19-year-old son, Jean-Claude. The problem was that he was constitutionally too young to be president. So Papa Doc's obedient assembly lowered the age requirement for the office from 40 to 20 and, for good measure, decreed that Jean-Claude was 21, not 19. The public voted on the new laws and approved them, 2,391,916 to 1. People wondered who the "1" was.

With preparations in place for his son to succeed him, Papa Doc's work was done. He died of heart failure on April 21, 1971, at the age of 64. His life had lasted about twice as long as that of the average Haitian.

Duvalier was canonized in a Voodoo ritual as "Loa-zz-Zo," joining the spirits of Dessalines, Toussaint, Christophe, Pétion, Estimé, and a pantheon of others. The day after Papa Doc died, Jean-Claude was inaugurated president-for-life. It was the 22nd, Papa Doc's lucky day of the month.

I seek not violence, I seek not reprisals, but I do not fear to carry them out whenever called for.
—FRANÇOIS DUVALIER

6

Baby Doc Comes of Age

Jean-Claude Duvalier did not appear in public on April 24, 1971, the official day of mourning for his father. The dictator's body lay in state beneath the glass lid of a rose-festooned coffin in the diplomatic reception room of the National Palace. The familiar thick-lensed horn-rimmed glasses were in place, and the body was clad in the usual black frock coat, white shirt, and white bow tie. There was a gold cross on the pillow to the left of the head, and a red leather copy of his *Memoirs of a Third World Leader.*

An honor guard of 22 members of the military stood at attention alongside the coffin as thousands of people paid homage to the man who had ruthlessly ruled Haiti for more than 13 years. The mourners who came to view the body were calm and orderly, displaying little emotion until they approached the body. Then they broke down. "Papa Doc! Papa Doc!" they cried. Some tried to throw themselves onto the coffin; others rolled around on the floor in spasms of grief. The hold Duvalier had on his superstitious people was palpable even in death. Many believed that Duvalier's spirit would rule through his son, Jean-Claude, who was immediately nicknamed "Baby Doc."

It's amazing that such a human being has been progressively taking more control. He's mastering it.
—SERGE FOURCAND minister of commerce and industry on Jean-Claude Duvalier's ascent to power

Jean-Claude and Simone Duvalier view Papa Doc's body as it lies in state during the April 24, 1971, funeral service. Nineteen-year-old Jean-Claude became president-for-life, but only after the Haitian assembly passed a law declaring him 21 years of age — just old enough to legally hold office.

Escorted by officers of the Haitian army, Jean-Claude Duvalier, the world's youngest chief of state, walks through the streets of Port-au-Prince four days after taking office. Baby Doc was advised by a 12-member cabinet appointed by his father before his death.

The Voodoo belief that Papa Doc was communicating with the people of Haiti through Baby Doc resulted in the first smooth governmental transition in Haitian history. Political analysts in North America and Europe, who played down the power of Voodoo in Haitian society and predicted anarchy and revolution after Papa Doc's death, were confounded. They could not believe that Jean-Claude, who enjoyed beautiful women, fast cars and motorcycles, jazz, and Haitian merengue music, could maintain power. Yet that was precisely what he did. The tall, light-skinned, 200-pound first-year law student, dressed in his father's traditional attire of black suit and white shirt, promised to continue the Duvalier "revolution" with the "same fierce energy and intransigence" as his father.

But whereas Papa Doc had a thirst for power and blood, Baby Doc had a hunger for money. Jean-Claude proved willing to open the Haitian economy to U.S. investment, and the White House accordingly embraced his regime as "more liberal" than his father's. Foreign corporations began relocating to Haiti because of the cheap labor and, in the process, kept the peasants' wages low in order to maximize profits. Thus with the return of investment came the return of foreign exploitation.

Pointing to the movement of foreign companies into Haiti, U.S. government aid agencies and lending institutions insisted Haiti was developing economically, even though the Haitian economy was in fact on the verge of collapse. Agriculture, the historic mainstay of the economy and the backbone of the Voodoo mountain culture, had been suffering from years of unchecked soil erosion and could no longer support the burgeoning population. By the late 1970s, the combites, the ancient village support system for more than 4.5 million rural peasants, began to crumble, forcing more and more farmers to seek refuge from starvation in the capital city or to leave the country entirely. Jean-Claude, who had never paid attention to the poverty that lay beyond the gates of the National Palace, ignored the mounting economic and social crisis.

Jean-Claude Duvalier was born in Port-au-Prince on July 3, 1951. He was a pampered child, yet he grew up an eyewitness to the brutal excesses of power and quickly learned the arts of graft, manipulation, and self-defense. He became an expert marksman with the pistol, rifle, and light machine gun (rumor had it that at age 13 he used a palace officer as a pistol target, fatally shooting him) and was proficient in judo and karate.

His academic performance, however, was less than stellar. After the Barbot kidnapping attempt, he was transferred to Saint-Louis de Gonzague, a Catholic school. Classmates called him "Basket-head," and by all accounts Jean-Claude was a lazy student: "He always passed all of his subjects," a Haitian schoolmate told a reporter for the *National Observer*, "but it was only because his instructors took pity. On themselves, not on Jean-Claude." He learned some Spanish and English at a European secondary school before graduating in June 1970 with a Haitian diploma that was the equivalent of an American community college degree. That fall he enrolled in the University of Haiti Law School and received scholastic counseling from the dean. Less than a year later, at age 19, he became president-for-life, the youngest chief of state in the world. It was a position he had not been prepared to fill but

I will continue the Revolution with my father's fierce energy.
—JEAN-CLAUDE DUVALIER

73

Duvalier in the uniform of the Leopard Battalion, the army unit he created to replace the Tontons Macoutes, which he disbanded in 1971. The move was one of the mild reforms Baby Doc instituted to induce the U.S. government to increase aid to Haiti. Mama Doc, his unofficial but paramount adviser, stands nearby.

a job he learned very quickly. "Some people are calling him 'the idiot son' but don't be fooled," one Haitian cautioned a *Life* magazine reporter in 1971. "That is exactly what they said about his father."

Upon becoming president, Jean-Claude appointed a new 12-member cabinet, whose ministers had been chosen by Papa Doc before he died. Among the appointees was the infamous Luckner Cambronne, by now the longest-surviving member of the Duvalier clique, who was named minister of interior, defense, and police. Other powerful figures in the background were Baby Doc's eldest sister, Marie-Denise, who continued in her role as secretary to the president, and his frail but commanding mother, Simone, whom he often referred to as "my inspiration." Together they formed a squabbling inner circle of advisers who made most of Baby Doc's initial decisions.

In his first major act as president, Baby Doc disbanded the Tontons Macoutes and restructured his security forces. Under the new arrangement the 650-man Leopard Battalion replaced the Macoutes, who either joined Baby Doc's security forces or retreated to their respective secret societies. The Leopards' official purpose was to fight communism, a theme the new regime felt would please the Americans, who had not yet restored aid. Its name was probably adopted from the Leopard secret society, a group known for its ability to create from tree bark a sort of truth serum called *ibok usiak owo*, meaning "a medicine for mentioning people." By adopting the Leopard name Duvalier may have been sending a message to the Haitian people that he, like his father before him, was keeping a close watch on them.

Still, the dismantling of the Tontons Macoutes and the promises of reform had their desired effect: The United States was impressed. "Haiti seems suddenly to have leapt from the 18th century to the 20th," wrote a *Washington Post* reporter five months after Baby Doc took over. Jean-Claude invited all exiles except "communists and troublemakers" to return to Haiti, commuted the death sentences of some political prisoners, started paying the country's debts to foreign lending agencies, and actively sought foreign aid.

Baby Doc's first political crisis occurred in August 1971 when a power struggle between Cambronne and Marie-Denise came to a head. It was widely believed that Marie-Denise had been the effective leader of the Haitian government since her father's death. But when Cambronne had his men arrest Marie-Denise's cousin-in-law for forging passports, she demanded that her brother choose between her and Cambronne. Duvalier chose Cambronne, and Marie-Denise flew back to Paris to join her husband.

Baby Doc sits expressionless as his chief minister, Luckner Cambronne (right), speaks to a European diplomat in 1972. Cambronne was one of Haiti's richest and most powerful men until Baby Doc, seeking to consolidate his own power, fired him a few months after this photo was taken.

A Haitian woman stitches baseballs at a factory owned by a U.S. manufacturer. Baby Doc encouraged foreign investment in Haiti, where 80-percent unemployment enabled companies to hire workers at extremely low wages, but the new factories did little to develop the Haitian economy.

Cambronne took over as the now 20-year-old president's chief decision maker, but things soon went sour for him. Baby Doc was basking in his role as "idol of his people" and visibly gaining confidence as the months passed. More and more he was at odds with Cambronne, who had become internationally infamous through his governing and business tactics. One of the chief extortionists for Papa Doc's Tontons Macoutes, Cambronne was involved in virtually every profitable business in Port-au-Prince. "If I were Cambronne, I'd watch it," a Haitian insider told a *Newsweek* reporter in May 1972. "In another three years, he may find that instead of being the Minister of Everything, he has become Minister of Nothing." Less than four months later Cambronne was fired. Many of his businesses were either closed or taken over by Baby Doc.

In the summer of 1973, one year after Cambronne's departure, Baby Doc's power became absolute. A fire in the palace armory set off a series of explosions under the president's bedroom window, evidently scaring him into staging a massive government reshuffling. When he was through, most of Papa Doc's old guard had been replaced. At age 22, after less than 3 years as president, Baby Doc was now firmly in the driver's seat. His chief adviser was his mother, whom peasants had begun calling "Mama Doc." Although frail and aging, Mama Doc still substantially influenced Jean-Claude's decisions, even to the point of passing judgment on his choice of girlfriends.

A seemingly more mature Baby Doc had emerged. He slimmed down somewhat and dispensed with the black-and-white attire of his father, preferring shiny sharkskin suits instead. He began to involve himself in the day-to-day work of running the government and seemed anxious to eliminate some of its more notorious excesses. Actual cabinet meetings were held, something that had been a rarity under his father, and cabinet ministers were required to work a full eight-hour day. Jean-Claude appeared to be trying to create a much-needed civil service.

Nevertheless, graft was still the chief purpose of the government apparatus. The legislature continued to act as a rubber stamp for the president-for-life, the press existed solely as a mouthpiece of the National Palace, opposition political groups and labor unions were allowed to exist only intermittently, and shakedowns remained a feature of commercial life. All of this occurred so that Baby Doc could pursue his practice of skimming public funds on an enormous scale. Jean-Claude siphoned into his personal bank accounts some $20 million in government revenue annually, most of it foreign aid from the United States. By 1975 the missing money — which could have been used for public-works projects, health care, or education — amounted to an estimated 40 percent of the Haitian government's total yearly expenditures.

This sort of money management did not demonstrate an overriding concern for the impoverished masses. But in the eyes of the U.S. government and the foreign investors and lenders, Haiti had taken great strides. Tourism had returned as a flourishing industry, and cheap labor had attracted 200 corporations, most of them American. The corporations set up small plants that assembled exports to the United States from materials that originally had come from the United States or elsewhere. By 1975 they had created 15,000 new jobs — a gigantic boost to a country with only 84,000 salaried workers out of a total population of 5.2 million — and pumped an estimated $100 million a year into the local economy. As a result, Haiti's economy began to grow, and Baby Doc raised the average wage from 70 cents to $1.30 a day. It was still not enough to live on, but it was nearly twice as much as workers had received under Papa Doc.

Nevertheless, the vast majority of the population remained unemployed, power and wealth continued to be concentrated in the hands of a few, and graft and corruption permeated Baby Doc's new economic structure. Critics of Haiti's labor policy called it "contemporary slavery." The list of U.S. corporations that profited from cheap peasant labor included many familiar names: the electronics firms TRW, Phillips, Motorola, Sylvania, and Allied Control; the clothing manufacturers Levi Strauss and MacGregor; and the sporting-goods makers Spald-

A Haitian hemp cutter returns from an 11-hour workday for which he earned a total of 40 cents. Baby Doc did little to stop the deterioration of Haitian agriculture, which in turn weakened the traditional structure of rural society.

A peasant gathers wood near a tree stump in a deforested Haitian landscape. By the late 1970s almost 95 percent of Haiti's once-vast forests were gone as a result of more than three centuries of uncontrolled cutting. The loss of trees resulted in severe soil erosion, which destroyed the nation's agriculture.

ing, Rawlings, and Wilson, which employed Haitian women to stitch baseballs. At 38 cents a dozen (roughly $1.33 a day), these women stitched enough American cowhide around Puerto Rican cores to make Haiti the largest producer of baseballs in the world.

But perhaps the saddest example of all was the impoverished Haitian sugarcane cutter. Each December before the annual sugar harvest, thousands of hungry peasants fought for the chance to board trucks headed for the Dominican Republic, where they could spend six months cutting cane (the Dominicans shunned the back-breaking cane-cutting jobs as degrading "Haitian work.") This flow of migrant workers, which involved 19,000 Haitians working at 12 plantations owned by the Dominican government, was administered jointly by Haiti and the Dominican Republic. The cane cutters were paid about $1.50 per ton cut; the average worker might cut 2 tons in a 16-hour day. They lived in makeshift camps adjacent to the sugarcane fields in shacks with no plumbing, running water, or electricity. Workers were routinely cheated at the scales, resulting in an incalculable loss of wages. In addition, every two weeks the workers were docked one dollar, which was turned over to the Haitian embassy as "compulsory savings"; they never saw the money again. Thus the sugar industry, which accounted for approximately two-thirds of the Dominican Republic's foreign exchange, was also built on the backs of Haitian laborers.

There were also thousands of illegal Haitian migrant workers, transported over the border by members of the Dominican military. Here there was no contract involved for the migrants, who toiled in squalid conditions providing the majority of the work force for private landowners such as the U.S.-based Gulf - Western corporation. The Haitians submitted to such migrant labor in the Dominican Republic simply because there was no work in Haiti.

Because of the inaccurate perception that Baby Doc was liberalizing his regime and promoting economic growth, foreign aid continued to pour in to Haiti. By the mid-1970s, the country was receiving more foreign aid per capita than any country in the world, and the United States was the largest single source. But the aid was of little help; the U.S. aid programs generally promoted the commercial health of American corporations, not the welfare of the Haitian people.

Other U.S. aid programs directly aimed at helping the Haitian peasant were often ill conceived. For example, in 1978 a swine fever epidemic wiped out more than half of Haiti's 1.2 million black pigs. The rest were slaughtered during a U.S.-backed pig eradication effort aimed at keeping the disease from spreading to other countries in the Western Hemisphere. The tough black Creole pigs were the peasants' main source of income; furthermore, they were

Three Haitians bring a small load of sugarcane to Port-au-Prince in 1973. The poverty of rural Haiti forced an enormous influx of peasants into the capital throughout the 1970s and early 1980s. Living in vast slums, their disaffection with Baby Doc's regime mounted in the 1980s.

the required sacrificial animal for some Voodoo rituals. The Haitian and U.S. governments replaced the black pigs with American Hampshire, Yorkshire, and Duroc pigs. Although the new pigs grew twice as fast, fetched twice the price, and yielded more meat and more piglets than the tough old Creole pigs, they could not adapt to the harsh conditions of Haitian life. They required imported feed and special sties that cost more money than the peasants had for their own food and shelter. The Haitian government eventually had to replace many of the delicate U.S. pigs with tough, semiwild ones from Jamaica.

But the most disastrous situation the nation faced was the loss through erosion of virtually all the topsoil on the entire Haitian side of Hispaniola, a problem too great for any amount of U.S. aid to solve. Over the generations hungry peasants had stripped the land of its trees in order to plant quick-growing crops and to make fires for warmth, cooking, and Voodoo ceremonies. By the late 1970s, Haiti, a land Christopher Columbus described as almost completely forested, had lost almost 95 percent of its original tree cover, ruining the delicate island ecosystem. With no trees or grass to hold Haiti's abundant rainfall, the soil washed down the

With the collapse of Haiti's agriculture, thousands of Haitian peasants sought work as seasonal laborers on sugar plantations in the Dominican Republic. There they worked for low pay under deplorable conditions; some of the plantations where they worked were owned by large U.S. corporations.

mountains and into the sea, choking off lakes, streams, reservoirs, and irrigation systems along the way. The land became infertile and agriculture came to a halt.

For centuries the soil had supported the economic, political, and social traditions of the countryside. Now the rural population started to flood into Port-au-Prince, hoping to land some of the scarce jobs in manufacturing. Under Papa Doc, Port-au-Prince's population doubled; under Baby Doc it doubled again to more than 1 million people, the vast majority of whom were poor. Nevertheless, American businessmen seemed blind to the problems the country faced. "We're very bullish on Haiti," a vice-president of American Airlines said to a *New York Times* reporter in March 1975. "The people are happy. There's no racial problem. Social restlessness isn't a positive attraction for tourists."

News of Baby Doc's perceived successes traveled rapidly to New York City's large Haitian community, where Michèle Bennett, who had been working as a secretary for a bedroom-slipper company, was intrigued. The last time she had seen Jean-Claude he was a fat schoolboy who, in her words, "used to pull my braids." She lost contact with him after her family, members of the mulatto elite and therefore fearful of Papa Doc, sent her away to a boarding school in Peekskill, New York. Michèle, a beautiful and willful young woman, moved back to Haiti in the late 1970s to seduce Baby Doc.

Their affair scandalized Port-au-Prince and in particular Mama Doc. Michèle was a divorcée with two sons, and it just so happened that her former husband was Alix Pasquet, the son of Alix Pasquet, Sr., the man who in 1958 had tried to oust Papa Doc. To make matters worse for Mama Doc, the whole capital city knew about the love affair. Stories of Michèle's sexual skills soon began circulating, as did rumors of her enlisting the help of a houngan who gave her a lotion to attract Jean-Claude. Whatever it was that she did to entice the young president-for-life, it worked. Against the wishes of his mother and just about everyone else in the inner circle, Jean-Claude proposed marriage.

Duvalier dances with his fiancée, Michèle Bennett, in 1980. Bennett moved back to Haiti from New York, where she had lived since she was a teenager, to pursue Baby Doc. Mama Doc was opposed to her son's affair with Bennett, a divorcée and a woman she suspected was scheming for power.

7

Televisions for the Slums

The wedding of Jean-Claude Duvalier and Michèle Bennett on May 27, 1980, was so lavish it made the *Guiness Book of World Records.* The bride wore a white designer gown and a matching headdress made of silk, and the ceremony was beamed to government televisions set up for the occasion throughout the slums of Port-au-Prince. After the formal "I dos," Jean-Claude kissed the bride, and $100,000 in fireworks lit up the sky.

With Jean-Claude's marriage to Michèle, his rule — which many had hoped was inching toward democracy or at least a more benevolent form of dictatorship — became bloodier and greedier. Together they stole millions of dollars and flaunted an opulent life-style in the midst of increasing poverty. As his greed consumed him, Duvalier crushed his opponents, letting up on the repression only when the American government was considering whether or not to renew aid programs.

When you are President and First Lady, you are like a mother and father to the people.
—MICHÈLE DUVALIER

Jean-Claude Duvalier and Michèle Bennett at their $3 million wedding ceremony on May 27, 1980. Next to Baby Doc sits his best man, former foreign minister Edner Brutus, and Mama Doc sits next to Bennett. Bennett soon stripped Mama Doc of most of her power.

Divisions within the Duvalier government soon became apparent. Papa Doc's old guard had lost ground to the rising class of mulatto businessmen linked to U.S. economic interests and to Michèle. The countryside was rife with rumors that the spirits were angry with Jean-Claude. A deepening conflict between the Roman Catholic church and the government increased discontent. The Tontons Macoutes reemerged, and it was not always clear whose side they were on. The country's economic, social, and political fabric was unraveling.

Within a year of her wedding, Michèle Bennett Duvalier, who privately referred to her husband as *"mon tonton,"* began to consolidate her power. She moved almost all of Jean-Claude's relatives out of the National Palace, took away the title first lady of the republic from Mama Doc, publicly castigated assemblymen and cabinet ministers, and spent millions of dollars in public funds to redecorate the immense two-story private apartment she shared with Jean-Claude in the palace. She built a private medical suite, a master bedroom and bath with gold fixtures, a refrigerated room to house her fur coats, and vaults to contain her extensive collection of designer jewels. Expensive chandeliers hung from the ceilings, and masterpieces of art lined the walls. The renovations cost $17 million, which came out of the funds earmarked for Haiti's armed forces.

The Duvaliers grew bolder in their siphoning of public funds. Baby Doc transferred vast sums of money outside the country through three of Haiti's national banks, and in December 1980 he skimmed $20 million of a $22 million International Monetary Fund loan within two days of its arrival. For her part, Michèle laundered money through government-owned businesses and skimmed funds from her favorite charity: the Michèle B. Duvalier Foundation. Once she staged a lavish charity ball to raise money for a clinic for "my poor people." Tickets cost $500 apiece, and 800 of them were sold. Like the wedding, the event was televised to the slum dwellers, who watched as a $30,000 necklace was raffled off. A total of $400,000 was raised, but none of the money ended up in the clinic's account.

The Bennett family also benefited from the Duvalier regime. Michèle's father, Ernest Bennett, acquired a few cargo planes and became one of Haiti's 25 exporters of coffee, and when finance minister Marc Bazin told the cabinet that Bennett owed an estimated $1 million in export taxes on his coffee beans, Michèle fired him. The Bennetts' business interests apparently were not confined to coffee. The *Washington Post* uncovered evidence that Bennett was the godfather of the cocaine trade in Haiti, and in 1982 Michèle's brother Frantz was arrested in Puerto Rico on drug-smuggling charges.

With the birth in 1983 of her son, François Nicolas, Michèle provided an heir apparent to the Duvalier dynasty. More and more Michèle was looking like the real power behind the throne. But whatever the extent of Michèle's influence, Jean-Claude was still the man the U.S. government dealt with in questions of foreign aid to Haiti, and he was careful to revise his game plan according to the political climate in Washington.

A group of Port-au-Prince Tontons Macoutes awaits instructions before the wedding ceremony. Baby Doc revived the Macoutes at the end of the 1970s and received their support, at least at first.

Duvalier and U.S. president Jimmy Carter's ambassador to the United Nations, Andrew Young, share a glass of wine at a state dinner at the National Palace in 1977. Carter's demand that Baby Doc respect human rights led him to allow opposition groups to function. Mama Doc reportedly responded by putting a hex on Carter.

Duvalier loosened his grip during the administration of U.S. president Jimmy Carter, who made human rights a major campaign issue, and tightened it again after the election of Ronald Reagan, who had thrown his support behind all anticommunist regimes regardless of their human-rights records. Between 1977 and 1979, pressure from the Carter administration had produced a brief democratic awakening in Haiti; political parties, trade unions, intellectual and cultural organizations, and an independent press were allowed to form. Mama Doc was so angered by the new liberal policies that she is reported to have put a Voodoo hex on Carter. But on November 28, 1980, just 24 days after Reagan's election, Duvalier's forces staged a crackdown. In a secret wave of arrests, Duvalier's police swept more than 200 human-rights activists, trade union organizers, journalists, doctors, lawyers, and development workers into jail. Many were brutally beaten. The chief of police described all of them as "national and international communist agitators."

The Reagan administration's response was mild. Official letters of protest from the American embassy were delivered to Haitian government officials several days after the crackdown on the democratic organizations. On December 10, 1980, a week after the letters were received, the OAS approved $148 million in aid to Haiti. The U.S. response, followed by the allocation of millions of dollars in aid, made it appear as though the White House was rewarding Duvalier for a job well done.

With formal political opposition silenced, hundreds of local Catholic parishes and Protestant missionary groups took the lead in pressing for change by providing social services and lobbying against the Duvalier regime. In December 1982 the government arrested and tortured a Catholic layworker, prompting a public letter of protest from the Haitian archbishop, who was related to Michèle Bennett. Two months later Pope John Paul II visited Haiti and publicly rebuked the government for "the injustice, the excessive inequality, the degradation of the quality of life, the misery, the hunger, the fear of many people."

As Michèle Duvalier keeps her distance, Baby Doc converses with Pope John Paul II in Haiti in 1983. In the early 1980s local priests and missionaries led the struggle for human rights in Haiti. During his visit the pope called for an end to repression of church activists and called on the regime to respect civil liberties.

In 1983 the U.S. Congress, before deciding whether to renew aid to Haiti, asked the State Department to certify that Haiti was making progress toward improving human rights. This prompted the Haitian government to create a figurehead human-rights commission, relax press censorship, and hold legislative elections a few months before certification was due. The elections were a sham — only government-supported candidates won — and Duvalier followed up by sending highly publicized letters to the minister of justice and the heads of the police, armed forces, and militia, ordering them to respect the legal rights of prisoners and to refrain from using torture. The U.S. State Department — as concerned with propping up the Haitian dictatorship as a buffer against Castro as it had been 25 years before — certified that Duvalier was improving the human-rights situation in Haiti.

It is often said that the first step toward a dictatorship's collapse occurs when it decides to offer a few token reforms; the oppressed citizens get a glimpse of what life might be like under a more liberal regime, and they get angry. So it was in Haiti. Duvalier's gestures of reform tantalized the urban poor, even after the abuses resumed.

U.S. Coast Guardsmen aboard a boat bringing Haitians to the United States illegally in 1981. Poverty and repression forced thousands of Haitians to crowd onto small, leaky boats to make the 580-mile trip to Florida. Those who were not drowned or forced to turn back were detained by U.S. immigration officials on arrival.

While the Duvaliers and their officials diverted millions of dollars in public funds into private overseas bank accounts, the majority of Haitians continued to live in poverty. By 1985, 80 percent of the population was illiterate, life expectancy 43 years, and the average income $333 per year.

On May 21, 1984, police beat to death a pregnant woman from Gonaïves, a bleak town 68 miles north of Port-au-Prince. Suddenly Haitians exploded. "Down with hunger! Down with misery! Down with Duvalier!" they chanted before storming the warehouses of a private American aid organization to get at the food stored inside. By the time Duvalier's troops quelled the riot with gunfire and machetes, at least 30 people were dead.

Many feared that Duvalier would stage another major crackdown after the reelection of President Reagan in November 1984, and they were right. Immediately after Reagan's victory, which ensured another four years of U.S. support for Baby Doc's dictatorship, a new wave of arrests and government violence swept Haiti. This time the church and the development institutions were the primary targets.

A detachment of uniformed Tontons Macoutes outside the National Palace in 1986. Duvalier lost the support of the Bizango secret society and thus the Macoutes, who believed that he was favoring the mulatto elite at the expense of the black majority. The withdrawal of their support would prove costly to Baby Doc.

The government announced that it had uncovered "a plot of Marxist-Leninist inspiration against the security of the state" and rounded up 37 agronomists, economists, and church-affiliated community-development workers. Duvalier released them six months later, and the U.S. State Department cited the move as one of the reasons it recertified aid to Haiti. It failed to mention that many of the prisoners had been severely tortured during their six months of detention.

The growing unrest prompted Baby Doc to revive the Tontons Macoutes as an official, uniformed branch of the military. The Macoutes were placed under the command of a six-member council of directors and not, as in the days of Papa Doc, under the leadership of local and regional Bizango gang lords like Zachary Delva. As a result, they did not seem as fierce and powerful as in years past. Meanwhile, the old Papa Doc Macoutes had maintained their existence as an underground paramilitary force controlled by the Bizango society leadership, which was becoming increasingly unhappy with the young Duvalier's promulatto policies and his marriage. The Bizango leaders believed that Michèle and her family had to go.

None of this was helping the vast majority of Haitians, for whom things were getting steadily worse. In 1977, Haiti had been the 25th-poorest nation in the world; in the early 1980s it was the 9th-poorest.

It was the poorest country in the Western Hemisphere and the poorest in the world outside of Africa. The misery and deprivation forced one out of every seven Haitians to emigrate to the United States, Canada, the Dominican Republic, the Bahamas, French Guiana, or the French Caribbean islands of Guadeloupe and Martinique. In 1988 there were an estimated 1 million Haitians living outside their native land, more than half of them in the United States.

The first wave of Haitian refugees emigrated to America after the election of Papa Doc in the late 1950s. They were mostly mulatto professionals who had come with immigration papers. In 1971, the year Baby Doc inherited the presidency, hundreds of poor Haitians began arriving illegally on American shores. Fleeing Haiti in leaky, overloaded sailboats, they often died in their attempt to escape Duvalier's oppression. Many, whose boats capsized or sank, never made it; photographs taken of the bodies, washing up on the shores of Florida, generated shock and sympathy throughout the United States.

But as the annual influx of Haitians climbed to 20,000 in 1980, the welcome mat was withdrawn. Despite many documented cases of persecution by the Duvalier regime, the Reagan administration insisted that the Haitians were fleeing economic conditions rather than political oppression and that therefore they were ineligible for political asylum under U.S. law. Those who continued to arrive were thrown into detention camps in Miami and Puerto Rico until U.S. officials could review their petitions for asylum, a process that could take a year or more.

> *I don't want to explain how our system worked.*
> —MICHÈLE DUVALIER when asked how Haitian government finances worked under Jean-Claude Duvalier

The plight of the Haitian boat people reached its height in June 1984, when the Coast Guard stopped a small wooden sailboat overloaded with 70 men, women, and children attempting to flee to Florida. As immigration officials stepped on board, the frightened refugees crowded to one side of the boat and it capsized. Twelve people drowned. The event focused international attention on the Haitian boat people, on U.S. foreign policy in the Caribbean, and on Duvalier's corrupt regime. For Baby Doc, the end was near.

8

New Blood

For the first time since the 1804 revolution, both rural and urban Haiti were crumbling. For generations 85 percent of the population had lived independently of the capital city, creating their own laws based on their own religion, values, and customs. But now exhausted soil, treeless mountains, lack of services, and marauding Tontons Macoutes had forced thousands of farmers off their property and away from their combites, and into the city or onto overloaded, ill-equipped boats bound for the United States.

Most who fled the countryside ended up in the poorest slum of Port-au-Prince: a place called *Cité Soleil*, which means, oddly, Sun City. Two hundred thousand people lived in this sprawling agglomeration of closet-sized lean-to shacks, made of cardboard and corrugated metal, into which entire families were crowded. There was no sewage system, no electricity, and no running water. During the rainy season the pathways of Cité Soleil were choked with human and animal waste. Those with no living quarters spent their lives on the pathways, finding food where they could, bathing and washing in polluted drainage ditches.

We are only asking for what we have clear documentary proof was taken. . . . We have checks and bank documents to show how these funds were transferred abroad from the Defense Ministry Budgetary and other government accounts.
—YANN COLIN
post-Duvalier Haitian
government lawyer
attempting to reclaim
embezzled funds

Haitians in the town of Saint-Marc celebrate the departure of Jean-Claude Duvalier on February 7, 1986. Baby Doc's flight prompted optimism for human rights in Haiti, but it soon became clear that the Duvalierist military remained in charge with no intention of making significant changes.

In the older portions of the city conditions were much better, yet still appalling by North American standards. On crowded, twisted streets most of the city's inhabitants engaged in subsistence commerce, selling everything they could find or, in some cases, steal. Measles, diarrhea, and tetanus were epidemic, and malnutrition was widespread.

Coping with these conditions helped to induce a new boldness among Haitians. Business, political, and religious leaders called for a democratic government and respect for human rights, and a spontaneous, broad-based but unorganized movement against the government sprang up. Such developments were reported widely in the North American and European press, but what went unreported was the biggest blow against Baby Doc's regime: the Bizango's withdrawal of its support. Jean-Claude had reversed his father's practice by courting the mulatto elite and foreign businessmen at the expense of the secret societies and their vast membership. The Bizango and other secret societies now operated independently of the government, and increasingly in opposition to it. Baby Doc had lost control.

An open sewer in Port-au-Prince's Cité Soleil shanty-town. The influx of rural peasants quadrupled the capital's population from 240,000 in 1961 to almost 1 million in 1986. Most of the newcomers lived in squalid slums, which became centers of opposition to the regime in Baby Doc's final days as president.

The Duvaliers' descent from power accelerated after July 22, 1985, when Jean-Claude staged a referendum vote on proposed amendments to the constitution reaffirming the institution of presidency-for-life, allowing the president to choose a successor, and providing for political parties only if they professed loyalty to his regime. The government claimed that 99.9 percent of the 2.4 million voters cast ballots in favor of the amendments.

Church officials charged that the election was a fraud, and the Haitian government responded harshly. One day after the election, assailants — allegedly Duvalier security forces — clubbed to death an 80-year-old Belgian missionary priest during what was officially labeled a robbery. This was followed by the arrest and expulsion of two other Belgian missionary priests and the director of the Catholic radio station. After the expulsions Duvalier launched a campaign against the church through the government-controlled press, which printed articles reminding Haitians of some of the more disgraceful chapters in church history, such as its

Soldiers close in on a looter at a food warehouse owned by CARE, a privately run relief agency, during antigovernment riots in Gonaïves in 1985. The Macoutes responded harshly to the food riots in the northern city, which spread to other parts of Haiti.

Townspeople hold a mock funeral for a local Macoutes leader in Leogâne in February 1986. When the Bizango and other Voodoo secret societies withdrew their support for Baby Doc, his rural Macoutes network collapsed and he was forced to give up power.

endorsement of slavery. Despite these attacks, the United States made no move to suspend any of its planned $52 million in aid to Haiti for 1986. And although the State Department condemned the expulsions, one of its officials was quoted in *Newsweek* as saying: "With all its flaws the Haitian government is doing what it can."

In November 1985 a new round of antigovernment rioting broke out in the ramshackle town of Gonaïves, where the former slaves of Saint Domingue had declared their independence from France in 1804. Located in the Artibonite Valley, an area that forms the heart of Bizango territory, Gonaïves was the site of the first demonstration against the Duvalier regime in 1984. "The people in the government in Port-au-Prince must cooperate with us," said Jean-Jacques Leophin, a Bizango emperor, to Wade Davis. "We were here before them, and if we didn't want them, they wouldn't be where they are. There are not many guns in the country, but those that there are, we have them."

Michèle Duvalier was in Paris spending $1.7 million on a shopping spree when the rioting began in Gonaïves. Hundreds of peasants, protesting rising food prices and fuel shortages, torched shops and the homes of government supporters, tore down a customs house, and ransacked a food warehouse of the private American aid group CARE.

By January the unrest had spread to almost every city in the country with the exception of Port-au-Prince, Duvalier's stronghold. Rioting in the towns of Petit-Goâve, Miragoâne, and Jérémie brought out the Haitian army and the Tontons Macoutes, who quashed the disturbances in a violent, machete-wielding frenzy. In an attempt to quell the protests, Baby Doc promised to cut the price of rice, canned milk, cooking oil, and diesel fuel by 10 percent. But it was too late. Antigovernment fliers circulated in Port-au-Prince exhorting citizens to "rise up against the misery that tears at our gut, against the hunger of the streets, and the famine in the countryside."

Haitians in Brooklyn, New York, celebrate the fall of Duvalier. More than 1 million Haitians had left the country by 1986, with most going to Miami, New York, Boston, and Montreal. Others went to the Bahamas and the French Caribbean territories of Guadeloupe, Martinique, and French Guiana.

The exiled Duvaliers and two of their children at their villa in the south of France. Jean-Claude, Michèle, and their entourage used the vast sums of money they embezzled while in power to live luxuriously in exile. In 1988 the Haitian government was seeking to recover more than $200 million through the French courts.

By January 1986, foreign banks, investors, and suppliers had either pulled out of the country or cut back on operations. The tourism industry, already crippled by the high incidence of AIDS among Haitians, was in ruins. The U.S. government signaled its abandonment of the Duvalier regime when the State Department suspended almost all aid to Haiti. As rioting spread to Port-au-Prince, businesses and factories closed their doors, and the Haitian economy came to a standstill. Rioters chanting "Down with Duvalier!" smashed car and store windows and constructed roadblocks from tires and burning garbage.

As the situation degenerated, Jean-Claude used a radio address to threaten Haitians with his father's kind of violence, although Jean-Claude couched his threat in expressions of sympathy. "I understand your impatience, your legitimate aspirations to improve your standard of living," he said, "but we should remember that disorder and anarchy could only aggravate the situation." Baby Doc made good on his veiled threat and unleashed the full power of the Macoutes, which had grown to 15,000 members and had regained some of the fearsome reputation it had enjoyed during the Papa Doc years.

Although only seven bodies of people killed during protests were found in city morgues, rumors abounded that the Macoutes had their own disposal site — a marsh 10 miles north of Port-au-Prince. A European priest said he had been to the site several times to search for bodies of parishioners and discovered fresh, shallow graves. "They bring the bodies in pickup trucks, throw them in pits, pour calcium on the bodies, and then cover them with a thin layer of soil," he said, explaining that "the police can't throw the bodies into the sea because they will come back [with the tide]."

A jubilant scene in front of the National Palace in Port-au-Prince five days after Baby Doc fled the country. The caretaker government he left behind, dominated by the military, promised free speech, free elections, the right to hold demonstrations, and an end to government corruption.

Police stand near the body of one of six people killed during an April 1986 rally in Port-au-Prince. The rally, attended by 10,000 people, had been held to commemorate the victims of the Duvalier regime. Government violence against civilians resumed soon after the departure of Baby Doc.

On February 2, 1986, Jean-Claude received his most ominous warning yet from the Bizango society. At the head of a dancing parade of 1,200 peasants in Saint-Marc, two men walked in mock mourning bearing a wooden coffin. "Jan Clod Min Place Ou," was the Creole inscription painted on the side of the casket: "Jean-Claude your place is here." The spectacle was an indication that Baby Doc had been found guilty of misdeeds by the Bizango council of elders. The final nail in the regime's coffin came when 10 Voodoo priests, called to the National Palace to advise Jean-Claude on how to deal with the unrest, said that they no longer supported him.

On Thursday night, February 6, Duvalier sent word to the U.S. embassy that he would end his 15-year rule. "The last service I could render my country," he said, "is to polarize all the antagonisms onto myself and disappear, thus preventing bloodshed."

Duvalier took care of the final details. He withdrew money from his bank accounts one last time, leaving the national treasury only $500,000 in available cash. Then he and Michèle threw a midnight champagne party for themselves and their friends, drove to the airport, and flew away aboard a U.S. Air Force cargo plane.

A woman prays before a crucifix in Port-au-Prince on November 28, 1987, the day before Haiti's first free presidential election since 1957. Some 2,500 *ti-legliz* (little churches) led the struggle for human rights in the nation both during and after the Duvalier regime.

Soldiers view the bodies of 2 of 14 people hacked to death at a Port-au-Prince polling station on November 29, 1987. Namphy and the army did nothing to stop election-day violence, in which scores were killed by Macoutes gangs. Namphy canceled the voting and rescheduled it for June 1988. Leslie Manigat won the 1988 election.

The delight over Duvalier's ouster was obvious. Crowds of celebrating Haitians danced in the streets of Port-au-Prince singing, "He flew away! He flew away!" Haitian exiles all over the world toasted the spirit of their countrymen. In Miami, Boston, and New York, which have the largest Haitian populations in the United States, some exiles claimed that their bags were packed and that they were ready to return home. But others were more cautious. "I want to go back," Philippe Georges, a 58-year-old mechanic living in Miami, told a *Newsweek* reporter, "but I must wait to see who is going to run things. The boy wasn't the only bad one in Haiti."

Duvalier had already decided who would run things. Before he left, he had chosen a six-man ruling council, composed of four military men and two civilians, to take over the government until a new president could be elected. Five of the six men were longtime supporters of the regime, including the council head, Lieutenant Colonel Henri Namphy, the 53-year-old chief of the armed forces. The only member of the interim government who was never associated with the Duvaliers was Gérard Gourgue, a 60-year-old lawyer, human-rights activist, and outspoken critic of the regime; he was undoubtedly chosen to give the new interim government credibility.

Some Haitians voiced serious concerns about Duvalier's hand-picked governing council. To diffuse the criticism, Namphy summarily abolished Baby Doc's assembly, disbanded the uniformed branch of the Tontons Macoutes, reopened the schools, announced that he would allow an independent press to operate, and promised to hold elections at some unspecified point in the near future. Namphy also removed some of the more obvious manifestations of the Duvalier family's hold on the nation by renaming the airport, nationalizing all of the Duvalier-Bennett properties and businesses, and burning the Duvaliers' red-and-black flag, resurrecting Haiti's old blue-and-red flag in its place.

Free of the threat of reprisals after 29 years of oppression, Haitians took out their hatred on everything that reminded them of the Duvaliers. They looted homes and businesses owned by members of the Duvalier clique and hunted down Tontons Macoutes and Voodoo leaders connected with the regime. Namphy and the military did nothing to contain the violence. Their only distinction was to find more than 200 pounds of cocaine at the clinic funded by the Michèle B. Duvalier Foundation.

Meanwhile, in France, the Duvaliers and their associates arrived in a fleet of rented limousines at the posh but isolated Hôtel de l'Abbaye in Talloiress, a village in the French Alps. All 45 rooms in the converted 16th-century monastery had been reserved by the Duvaliers for $3,000 a day. The French government said the Duvaliers could stay for a maximum of one week, but as country after country turned down Jean-Claude's requests for permanent asylum, Baby Doc announced that he would seek permanent refugee status through the French courts. "At no moment was I given to understand that my stay in France was temporary," Duvalier said. "If I had believed that the only country in the world which I feel close to would not welcome me, then I would never have given up power."

> *Flee Haiti? Why do you say we were fleeing Haiti? The President and I decided it was time to leave. Nobody can say we had to leave Haiti. My husband had all the honors when he was leaving.*
> —MICHÈLE DUVALIER

Eventually the French government relented and allowed the Duvaliers to remain in the country but confined their movement to a 30-mile stretch along the Riviera, where the Duvaliers rented a luxurious villa; there they settled into a life of exile, sharing the compound with their relatives, including Michèle's first husband, Alix Pasquet. "People resent the Duvaliers' presence here," said Graham Greene, author of *The Comedians* and the Duvaliers' new neighbor. "The irony that they of all people should wind up in this area. Who could have imagined?"

In an interview published in *Vanity Fair* magazine in December 1986, Michèle blamed "that horrible American press" for her husband's fall and complained of spending her time in exile "unable to sleep, unable to concentrate on novels, really just watching the TV news. I'm up till 3 A.M. doing crosswords. And every 15 days I give Jean-Claude a manicure." She reflected on the country she and her husband had once ruled. "Haiti is so terrible now, since we left. It is anarchy. There are no laws, the people are running wild, there are 200 candidates for president."

Back in Haiti, events had indeed devolved into anarchy. In the first weeks after the Duvaliers fled, 100 Voodoo houngans, mambos, and loups garous, believed to have supported the regime, were shot or hacked to death, and a brief but vicious religious war erupted between Christians and Voodooists (significantly, there were no deaths reported in the Artibonite Valley, the stronghold of the powerful Bizango society). During the chaos, Namphy announced that former members of the Duvalier regime would not be prosecuted for human-rights abuses; the chiefs of Baby Doc's secret police and of the Tontons Macoutes were allowed to leave the country. Gérard Gourgue resigned from the governing council in protest, leaving Namphy and the military in charge of Haiti. More strikes, demonstrations, and riots broke out.

After two attempts at holding presidential elections during which more than 500 people died, including two presidential candidates, Namphy and the military elevated a political unknown to the pres-

idency. On January 17, 1988, Leslie F. Manigat, a 57-year-old former exile and political science professor, became president in an election rigged in his favor. Nevertheless, in his first speech he hinted that he would restrain the military and promised to mend the historical rift between black and mulatto. "I think the Haitian people need and deserve a democracy," he said. "I will not be in any case an instrument for the return of dictatorship to Haiti."

In June 1988, Manigat was deposed in a military coup after he had tried to reorganize the army and fire Namphy. Again Namphy took over and ruled by decree; again the Duvalierist military was in charge. Haiti remained a poor, backward nation ruled by a

Army general Henri Namphy, Baby Doc's hand-picked successor, in 1986. Though Namphy promised reforms and elections, the army and the Macoutes continued to terrorize the population. Some 500 people were killed during the campaign leading up to the presidential election scheduled for late 1987.

A woman in Port-au-Prince in
1988. Namphy overthrew
Manigat, the elected president, in September 1988.
One month later Namphy was
ousted by a former top
Duvalier aide, General Prosper Avril, and a young sergeant, Joseph Hébreux. They
promised elections by 1991;
Haiti remained hopelessly
impoverished.

dictator whose military regularly terrorized the civilian population. In September 1988 a group of machete-wielding Tontons Macoutes stormed a Roman Catholic church during a mass led by a priest who was a leading critic of the government's human-rights abuses. Twelve people were killed and 77 were wounded. Over the next few days five men and one woman claiming to have been among the attackers appeared on radio and television to say that any other critics of the government could expect the same treatment. Namphy did nothing.

A week later there was another coup. This time Namphy was overthrown and replaced by army general Prosper Avril. In the 1960s Avril had been one of Papa Doc's advisers, and in the 1970s and 1980s he was Baby Doc's money manager; it was believed that Avril masterminded the transfer of hundreds of millions from the public treasury into Jean-Claude's private accounts in overseas banks. But although Avril was now the president of Haiti, the coup was apparently led by a 27-year-old army sergeant, Joseph Hébreux, who seemed to share power in the new government. While sergeants and corporals arrested their officers and mobs hunted down and killed Macoutes in the streets, Hébreux and Avril declared their support for democracy and vaguely promised elections within two and half years. No one knew for certain whether they were sincerely devoted to democratic principles or merely making empty pledges to convince the American government to restore aid. Some even believed that Hébreux and Avril were puppets, manipulated by behind-the-scenes army officers.

Whatever the case, with the Duvalierist military still in charge, there was little hope for Haiti. Despite more than $600 million in foreign aid during Baby Doc's regime, conditions in Haiti on the eve of the 1990s were much the same as they had been for generations. The country that had fought so bravely for its independence 200 years before now found itself more dependent than ever on the outside world, a situation that promised to give rise to even greater anger and discontent within Haiti. The age-old cycle of poverty and repression, personified by the Duvaliers, had continued.

Further Reading

Davis, Wade. *The Serpent and the Rainbow.* New York: Warner, 1985.

Diederich, Bernard, and Al Burt. *Papa Doc.* New York: McGraw-Hill, 1969.

Dunham, Katherine. *Island Possessed.* New York: Doubleday, 1969.

Foster, Charles R., and Albert Valdman, eds. *Haiti Today and Tomorrow: An Inter-disciplinary Study.* Lanham, MD: University Press of America, 1984.

Gringas, Jean-Pierre O. *Duvalier: Caribbean Cyclone.* New York: Exposition Press, 1967.

Hinkle, Warren, and William Turner. *The Fish Is Red: The Story of the Secret War Against Castro.* New York: Harper & Row, 1981.

Honorat, Jean-Jacques. *The Political Economy of the Refugee Crisis.* New York: Queens College Institute of Haitian Studies, 1982.

James, C. L. R. *The Black Jacobins.* New York: Vintage, 1963.

Laguerre, Michel. *Politics and Voodoo Still a Potent Combination in Haiti.* New York: Macmillan, 1988.

———. *Voodoo Heritage.* Beverly Hills, CA: Sage, 1980.

Maguire, Andrew, and Janet Welsh Brown. *Bordering on Trouble: Resources and Politics in Latin America.* Bethesda, MD: Adler & Adler, 1986.

Schmidt, Hans. *The United States Occupation of Haiti: 1915–1934.* New Brunswick, NJ: Rutgers University Press, 1971.

Sunshine, Catherine A. *The Caribbean: Survival, Struggle, and Sovereignty.* Boston: South End Press, 1985.

Tate, Robert J. *Haiti: Land of Poverty.* Lanham, MD: University Press of America, 1982.

Williams, Eric. *From Columbus to Castro: The History of the Caribbean, 1492–1969.* New York: Harper & Row, 1970.

Chronology

April 14, 1907	François Duvalier born in Port-au-Prince, Haiti
1937	Dominican dictator Rafael Trujillo orders the massacre of 20,000 Haitian cane cutters migrating to his country in search of work
1946	Dumarsais Estimé is elected president; appoints Duvalier director of public health
1949	Duvalier becomes minister of public health and labor
May 1950	Colonel Paul Magloire deposes President Estimé in a bloodless coup
July 3, 1951	Jean-Claude Duvalier born in Port-au-Prince
Sept. 22, 1957	Duvalier elected president
July 1958	Forms the Tontons Macoutes
1959	Suffers a heart attack; Clément Barbot, chief aide to Duvalier, directs the defeat of a Cuban invasion force
1960	Duvalier jails Barbot for 16 months
April 1961	Is unconstitutionally reelected president of Haiti
June 14, 1964	Declares himself president-for-life
Jan. 1971	Haitian constitution amended to allow Duvalier to choose his successor
April 21, 1971	François Duvalier dies
April 22, 1971	Jean-Claude Duvalier is inaugurated; disbands the Tontons Macoutes
1980	Stages a massive crackdown on human rights proponents, development workers, and journalists
May 21, 1984	First widespread demonstration against the Duvalier regime
Jan. 1986	Duvalier declares a state of siege.
Feb. 7, 1986	Flees to France; Henri Namphy takes control of the government of Haiti

Index

Erin Condit is a graduate of the Columbia University Graduate School of Journalism in New York City with an interest in both the print and broadcast media. A former news director at a CBS network affiliate station, she has produced two film documentaries. In 1987 she won the John J. McCloy Fellowship in journalism.

Arthur M. Schlesinger, jr., taught history at Harvard for many years and is currently Albert Schweitzer Professor of the Humanities at City University of New York. He is the author of numerous highly praised works in American history and has twice been awarded the Pulitzer Prize. He served in the White House as special assistant to Presidents Kennedy and Johnson.

PICTURE CREDITS

AP/Wide World Photos: pp. 2, 14, 18, 25, 41, 44, 51, 52, 58, 60, 65, 67, 68, 74, 79, 81, 82, 86, 87, 98, 101; The Bettmann Archive: pp. 22, 24, 30; Wade Davis: pp. 48, 80; *Haiti Observateur*/Alix Auberge: p. 97; *Haiti Observateur*/Magot Granitas: p. 75; *Haiti Observateur*/Dave Healey: p. 85; Immigration and Naturalization Service: p. 88; National Archives: pp. 28, 29; Organization of American States: pp. 27, 34, 37, 54; Reuters/Bettmann Newsphotos: pp. 92, 96, 100, 102, 105; Donna Sinisgalli: p. 21; Maggie Steber: pp. 26, 35, 78, 90, 94, 95, 106; Sygma: p. 77; UNICEF/Maggie Black: p. 15; UNICEF/Nicole Touounji: p. 89; UPI/Bettmann Newsphotos: pp. 12, 16, 32, 39, 42, 46, 50, 55, 56, 63, 70, 72, 76, 99